MUSIC OF THE UNITED STATES OF AMERICA

Richard Crawford, Editor-in-Chief
Dorothea Gail, Executive Editor

---

1   Ruth Crawford: *Music for Small Orchestra (1926); Suite No. 2 for Four Strings and Piano (1929)*

2   Irving Berlin: *Early Songs, 1907–1914*

3   Amy Beach: *Quartet For Strings (In One Movement), Op. 89*

4   Daniel Read: *Collected Works*

5   *The Music and Scripts of "In Dahomey"*

6   Timothy Swan: *Psalmody and Secular Songs*

7   Harrigan and Braham: *Collected Songs, 1873–1896*

8   Lou Harrison: *Selected Keyboard and Chamber Music, 1937–1994*

9   Harry Partch: *Barstow (1968)*

10 Thomas Wright "Fats" Waller: *Performances in Transcription, 1927–1943*

11 *Writing American Indian Music: Historic Transcriptions, Notations, and Arrangements*

12 Charles Ives: *129 Songs*

13 Leo Ornstein: *Quintette for Piano and Strings, Op. 92*

14 Dudley Buck: *American Victorian Choral Music*

15 Earl "Fatha" Hines: *Selected Piano Solos, 1928–1941*

16 David Moritz Michael: *Complete Wind Chamber Music*

17 Charles Hommann: *Surviving Orchestral Music*

18 Virgil Thomson and Gertrude Stein: *Four Saints in Three Acts*

19 Florence Price: *Symphonies nos. 1 and 3*

20 *Songs from "A New Circle of Voices": The Sixteenth Annual Pow-wow at UCLA*

21 John Philip Sousa: *Six Marches*

22 *The Ingalls Wilder Family Songbook*

23 George Frederick Bristow: *Symphony no. 2 in D Minor, op. 24 ("Jullien")*

24 Sam Morgan's Jazz Band: *Complete Recorded Works in Transcription*

25 Mary Lou Williams: *Selected Works for Big Band*

MARY LOU WILLIAMS

SELECTED WORKS FOR
BIG BAND

Edited by Theodore E. Buehrer

Recent Researches in American Music • Volume 74

Music of the United States of America • Volume 25

Published for the
American Musicological Society
by

A-R Editions, Inc.
Middleton, Wisconsin

Published by A-R Editions, Inc.
8551 Research Way, Suite 180
Middleton, Wisconsin 53562

© 2013 American Musicological Society

Printed in the United States of America

ISBN 978-0-89579-762-9
ISSN 0147-0078

Frontispiece: Mary Lou Williams. The Mary Lou Williams Collection, Institute of Jazz
Studies, Rutgers University; used by permission.

Permission to publish the compositions was granted by the Mary Lou Williams Foundation,
Inc. DBA Cecilia Music Publishing Co.

Publication of this edition has been supported by a grant from the National Endowment
for the Humanities, an independent federal agency. Any views, findings, conclusions, or
recommendations expressed in this publication do not necessarily reflect those of the
National Endowment for the Humanities.

♾ The paper in this publication meets the minimum requirements of American National
Standard for Information Sciences—Permanence of Paper for Printed Library Materials,
ANSI Z39-48-1992.

To Emma
Who I hope will, like Mary Lou Williams,
remain focused on her passions
and not let anyone tell her what she can't do.

CONTENTS

FOREWORD

Music of the United States of America (MUSA), a national series of scholarly editions, was established by the American Musicological Society (AMS) in 1988. In a world where many nations have gathered their proudest musical achievements in published scholarly form, the United States has been conspicuous by its lack of a national series. Now, with the help of collaborators, the AMS presents a series that seeks to reflect the character and shape of American music making.

MUSA, planned to encompass forty volumes, is designed and overseen by the AMS Committee on the Publication of American Music (COPAM), an arm of the society's Publications Committee. The criteria foremost in determining its contents have been: (1) that the series as a whole reflect breadth and balance among eras, genres, composers, and performance media; (2) that it avoid music already available through other channels, duplicating only where new editions of available music seem essential; and (3) that works in the series be representative, chosen to reflect particular excellence or to represent notable achievements in this country's highly varied music history.

The American Musicological Society's collaborators in the national effort that has brought MUSA to fruition include the National Endowment for the Humanities in Washington, D.C., which has funded MUSA from its inception; Brown University's Music Department in Providence, Rhode Island, which provided the project's original headquarters; the University of Michigan School of Music, where, since 1993, MUSA has made its home; A-R Editions, Inc., the publisher on behalf of AMS, of the MUSA series; and the Society for American Music, which, through its representative to COPAM, has provided advice on the contents of MUSA.

Richard Crawford, Editor-in-Chief

ACKNOWLEDGMENTS

The completion of a project such as this is impossible without the help of many people. I would like to thank Editor-in-Chief Richard Crawford and the Executive Editors I have worked with at MUSA: Dorothea Gail, James Wierzbicki, and Mark Clague, who have each guided this edition through its various stages. I am thankful that they gave this project its initial approval, and their patient and thoughtful insights along the way were appreciated as well, making this volume much stronger than I could have accomplished alone. Their work was aided by editorial staff and out-side readers who, though they remained nameless to me, helped me to refine subsequent drafts of each edition and the accompanying essay, and I thank them as well.

Gaining access to archival material and manuscripts was crucial to the success of this project, and for that I must thank the helpful people at the Institute of Jazz Studies at Rutgers University-Newark, home of the Mary Lou Williams Collection. Special thanks to Annie Kuebler (d. August 2012) and Tad Hershorn, both of whom played important roles in the archiving of this collection, and to Dan Morgenstern, the (now-retired) Director of the Institute of Jazz Studies. Each of them, and the entire staff, welcomed me and encouraged me in my research, providing me with unusual access to the collection, helpful secondary resources, and sage advice. They were also instrumental in introducing me to Father Peter O'Brien, S.J., the Executive Director of the Mary Lou Williams Foundation and Williams's manager for the last almost-twenty years of her career. Father O'Brien is a champion of Williams's music and her career, and has been very supportive of my work from the beginning. I am thankful for his acute memory of Williams's career, for his insights about her music, for his patient answers to my many, sometimes extremely detailed questions that came up along the way, and most of all for his friendship. Mary Lou Williams's manuscripts also reside in the Duke Ellington Collection in the Archive Center at the Smithsonian National Museum of American History in Washington, D.C., as well as the Benny Goodman Papers at the Irving S. Gilmore Music Library at Yale University. The librarians at both institutions were extremely helpful and accommodating in providing me with the archived manuscripts and documents I needed.

The edition would not have gotten off the ground without the support of the National Humanities Center in the Research Triangle, NC, during my sabbatical year. The superb facilities at which I was in residence, their wonderful staff and resources available to Research Fellows, and the stimulating atmosphere surrounding the NHC provided long blocks of time and logistical support needed to dig in to this project. Special thanks to Geoffrey Harpham, Director, and Kent Mullikin, (now-retired) Deputy Director, for taking interest in this project and inviting me to be a Research Fellow for the 2006–7 year. Additionally, during the course of the residency, they, along with James Ketch, Director of the North Carolina Jazz Repertory Orchestra and Chair of the Jazz Studies Department at the University of North Carolina-Chapel Hill, encouraged and supported a concert of the editions (performed by the NCJRO) that appear in this volume that was hosted at the NHC. For me, this concert allowed Williams's music to come to life rather than merely residing on manuscript paper, in my computer's hard drive, or inside my head. The process of creating performable editions and bringing them to fruition for an audience that included members of Williams's family (including her two surviving sisters) was a rewarding experience that I will always cherish.

At various stages I consulted colleagues to assist me or offer advice on a specific aspect of the project. To Henry Martin and Andrew Homzy, thank you for encouraging my initial ideas about the potential of this MUSA volume. To Tammy Kernodle and Richard Domek, thank you for weighing in on biographical and transcription issues. And to my Music Department colleagues at Kenyon College, thank you for the big and small ways that you have encouraged and supported my work on this volume over the last several years.

I am thankful to the music students at Kenyon College, particularly those in the Kenyon Jazz Ensemble, for taking an interest in the big band music of Mary Lou Williams and reading through versions of these editions with me. Thanks also go to Robert Grabill, class of 2005, who during an independent study worked with me on early drafts of what would eventually become complete transcriptions that appear in this volume.

Finally, I am thankful to my wife, Leslie, and my three children for their patience and understanding every time my work on this volume took me away from time I could have spent with them. I am grateful for your love and support as I have seen this project through to completion!

Theodore E. Buehrer

MARY'S IDEAS: BIG BAND MUSIC BY MARY LOU WILLIAMS

A WOMAN'S PLACE IN NARRATIVES OF JAZZ

Careful listeners and readers need to spend very little time perusing Mary Lou Williams's solo piano recordings, or her manuscripts of big band compositions and arrangements, to realize her immense talent. A two-time Guggenheim Fellow later in her life, Williams spent her career honing her craft as a pianist, composer, and arranger, performing and having her music performed for audiences around the world. Yet questions emerge immediately: why has the story of this gifted musician been obscured for so long? Why have jazz historians generally avoided serious consideration of her music and her contributions to jazz, even as she garnered praise and respect from her peers? One obvious answer is that Mary Lou Williams was a woman performing and writing in the male-dominated field of jazz music whose abilities enabled her to defy the conventional gender roles implicit in the jazz narratives of her day. According to this view, women in jazz were rare, women pianists rarer still, and women who, besides their superiority as players, could also compose and arrange first-class music for big band and combo were simply unheard of.[1] Yet Duke Ellington famously described Williams as "perpetually contemporary," going on to say that "[h]er writing and performing are and have always been just a little ahead throughout her career."[2] Similar words of admiration can be found in articles on, interviews of, and autobiographies by many of Williams's contemporaries. Their insider's knowledge of the music and Williams's place in it speaks with authority.

In the last twenty years, jazz scholars have begun to re-examine long-held views of the music's history. The common narrative underpinned by these traditional views, which some of these scholars have referred to as the "dominant jazz discourse" or the "jazz tradition," has pervaded jazz historical writing for decades, which in turn has influenced readers' perceptions of jazz history. The narrative proceeds along these lines:

---

1. Kernodle offers a similar explanation in her biography of Mary Lou Williams, *Soul on Soul: The Life and Music of Mary Lou Williams* (2004). Kernodle also provides a second reason for Williams's exclusion from most jazz historical narratives: her piano style, composing style, and arranging style defied categorization. Williams mastered each new style from the 1930s into the 1970s, and her arrangements similarly evolved with the passage of time (see Kernodle, *Soul on Soul*, 2, for this discussion).

2. Ellington, *Music is My Mistress*, 169. This is not to suggest that jazz historians have ignored Williams. While by no means intended to be exhaustive, a search through a dozen or so jazz history books, old and new, reveals that most historians at least provide a brief biographical sketch and a summary of Williams's musical endeavors, and that the more recent the edition, the more information is included. Of special note are *Jazz: A History*, by Tirro (1993), and *Jazz: The First 100 Years*, by Martin and Waters (2011), both of which provide extensive treatment of Williams and her work.

the history of jazz is marked by a number of significant "great men" who played and crystallized the music of their time into a style embraced by many contemporaries, while some introduced changes that helped the music incorporate a newer style; the stylistic evolution of jazz takes a "straight-line" approach from its inception until about 1950, with style changes more or less marked by decade; and since 1950 new jazz styles, still unfolding by decade, have developed simultaneously with other styles. This stylistic pluralism has persisted to the present day. Tracing the tradition that has produced this narrative through a systematic examination of jazz historiography constitutes a study in and of itself, but it may be summarized by noting some of the seminal works in which it has appeared.[3] The 1950s in particular saw a number of writings that helped to formulate this paradigm, among them Barry Ulanov's *A History of Jazz in America* (1952), Marshall Stearns's *The Story of Jazz* (1956), and Leonard Feather's *The Book of Jazz* (1957). As the academy embraced the study of jazz increasingly during the 1960s, 1970s, and beyond, more histories emerged with style delineation and a focus on the great innovators as points of emphasis. These histories include such scholarly research works as Gunther Schuller's *Early Jazz: Its Roots and Musical Development* (1968) and Martin Williams's *The Jazz Tradition* (1970), as well as jazz history textbooks aimed at undergraduate readers, such as Joachim Berendt's *The Jazz Book* (1974), James Lincoln Collier's *The Making of Jazz: A Comprehensive History* (1978), and Mark Gridley's *Jazz Styles* (1978).[4]

If these works represent some of the leading purveyors of the traditional narrative, that narrative has seen challenges in the last two decades in a number of related fields, including the study of race theory, as well as sociological, critical, cultural, and gender studies.[5] Though jazz historiography is not a primary focus of my work, a brief discussion of the challenges to the traditional jazz narrative offered in recent years by those interested in gender and jazz will help to provide a framework for the work offered here, which is primarily musicological. The traditional jazz narrative made little room for women. According to this view, jazz is assumed to be a man's music because the musicians assumed to be "the best" are male. Where women surface in this history of jazz, they are typically vocalists, occasionally pianists, and rarely instrumentalists of other types. Except for singers, who often fronted otherwise all-male big bands or combos, women rarely played with men. And, except for the singers, they were likely to be judged by how masculine they sounded when they did play. As a convenient case in point, Mary Lou Williams's piano performances were often compared to those of her male counterparts. A French critic writing in the 1930s asserted, "Her style derives from the James P. Johnson and Fats Waller style, but is much more fantastic and ardent . . . Mary Lou Williams' playing is like that of a man; one would never guess that it was a woman playing."[6]

In the 1980s, three works on gender and jazz were published that began to dispel the notion that women did not—or could not—play jazz music. These books, by Sally Placksin, Linda Dahl, and D. Antoinette Handy, moved the stories of a number of women jazz musicians out of the footnotes of the jazz tradition, and brought their perspectives, their experiences, and their stylistic development into the open.[7] More

---

3. For good starting points in jazz historiography, see, for example, DeVeaux, "Constructing the Jazz Tradition"; and Tucker and Jackson, "Jazz."

4. Many of these works have been published in newer editions; the dates given refer to their first editions.

5. The bibliography of work that examines jazz and jazz history from perspectives outside of the traditional narrative (what has been called the "New Jazz Studies") is growing, but it began in the 1960s with the publication of Jones's *Blues People* (1963). Two more recent samples of challenges to the jazz historical narrative in separate volumes edited by Gabbard are *Jazz Among the Discourses* (1995) and *Representing Jazz* (1995).

6. Panassié, *Hot Jazz*, 118.

7. Handy, *Black Women in American Bands and Orchestras* (1981); Placksin, *American Women in Jazz: 1900 to the Present; Their Words, Lives and Music* (1982); Dahl, *Stormy Weather: The Music and Lives of a Century of Jazzwomen* (1984).

Theodore E. Buehrer

recently, other authors, most notably Sherrie Tucker, have furthered this work on gender and jazz.[8] In her work, Tucker goes beyond including women jazz musicians in the commonly held narrative as "exceptional" women jazz musicians, and even beyond the study of women or gender in jazz music. Tucker's approach is to study jazz in the field of gender (borrowing Joan Scott's terminology).[9] In Tucker's words,

> A study of jazz on a field of gender (as a field of power) may yield insights into how style hierarchies, star systems, club policies, hipness barometers, etc., were established by recording companies, music publishers, jazz journalists, and historians . . . I am interested in how ideas about jazz and gender affect each other, how jazz meanings have been structured by (and structure) historically and culturally specific ideas about femininity and masculinity.[10]

To that end, Tucker's *Swing Shift: "All-Girl" Bands of the 1940s* tells the stories of these bands, disrupting the prevailing notion that jazz music of that time (i.e., the Swing Era) was men's music. Presenting a gendered analysis of this period of jazz history, Tucker demonstrates ways in which both men's and women's understandings of gender played a role in the music and culture of the time, and she provides a new way of thinking about its narrative.

As noted, gendered study of jazz is but one of several fields of inquiry in which recent work has been done that challenges the traditional jazz-historical narrative. It provides a convenient point of departure for helping to understand the subject of this work: jazz pianist, composer, and arranger Mary Lou Williams (1910–81). Unlike the subjects of Tucker's book (e.g., the Darlings of Rhythm, the Sweethearts of Rhythm, the Prairie View Co-eds, et al.), Williams did not pursue a career in all-girl bands. Indeed, she preferred, and made the deliberate choice, to play with men when possible. When producer Leonard Feather put together a few recording dates for Williams and an all-girl combo in 1945 and 1946, she was wary of Feather's choice of other musicians for the dates for fear that the recordings might be viewed as mere novelties. Biographer Linda Dahl explains that Williams "did not disparage their musicianship publicly . . . But she was frankly wary about the wisdom of choosing sidemen [sic] on the basis of gender."[11] After the first recording session, Williams remained lukewarm about pursuing more recordings with the all-girl combo, saying, "It was the cattiest session I'd ever encountered; the girls talked more music than they played."[12] This comment suggests that Williams herself had internalized sexist attitudes that swirled around her male-dominated musical world. Further evidence can be observed in her statement about the men she played with throughout her career: "You've got to play, that's all. They don't think of you as a woman if you can really play . . . Working with men, you get to think like a man when you play. You automatically become strong, though this doesn't mean you're not feminine."[13] But this is not to suggest that Williams looked down on other women musicians. To the contrary, two of Williams's

---

8. See especially Rustin and Tucker, eds., *Big Ears: Listening for Gender in Jazz Studies* (2008); Sherrie Tucker, "Big Ears: Listening for Gender in Jazz Studies," (2001–2), and *Swing Shift: "All-Girl" Bands of the 1940s* (2000). For other relatively recent examples of work on gender and jazz, also see Ake, ed., *Jazz Cultures* (2002), containing his essay "Regendering Jazz: Ornette Coleman and the New York Scene in the Late 1950s"; Monson, "The Problem with White Hipness: Race, Gender, and Cultural Conceptions in Jazz Historical Discourse" (1995); Elworth, "Jazz in Crisis, 1948–1958: Ideology and Representation" (1995); Gabbard, "Signifyin(g) the Phallus: 'Mo' Better Blues' and Representations of the Jazz Trumpet" (1992).

9. Scott, "Gender: A Useful Category of Historical Analysis" (1986).

10. Sherrie Tucker, "Big Ears," 387.

11. Dahl, *Morning Glory: A Biography of Mary Lou Williams* (1999), 181. These sessions can now be heard on Classics 1050 (CD) and Classics 1021 (CD).

12. Ibid. Despite Williams's lukewarm response to the experience, the trio of Williams, June Rotenburg (bass), and Marjorie Hyams (drums) recorded two more studio dates (the second added guitarist Mary Osborne), and the trio performed in the 1947 Concerts in Jazz Series at Carnegie Hall.

13. McPartland, "Mary Lou," 12.

early role models were pianists Lovie Austin and Lil Hardin Armstrong, and she maintained friendships with many women musicians throughout her career. For example, Williams recalled in later years that she had been friends with many "terrific" women musicians working in Kansas City during her time there in the 1930s. What set Williams apart in Kansas City, and indeed throughout her career, is that she was "unique being with the band, the all-male band."[14]

During the last two decades Williams's career has begun to garner far more attention than ever before.[15] Along with increased public interest, jazz scholars have begun to reexamine her place in jazz history and her contributions as both a pianist and a composer/arranger. To this point, however, scholarly focus on Williams's music mostly has been limited to her large-scale compositions (e.g., Catholic masses or the multi-movement *Zodiac Suite*), while the music she wrote for big bands and, to a lesser extent, jazz combos, has mostly escaped scrutiny.[16] If Williams's gender helps to explain why this music has been overlooked, another reason is that, until recently, few jazz scholars have focused on analysis of pre-bebop big band music; much of the jazz music that has been analyzed from a musicological or theoretical perspective has involved improvised solo performances.[17] However, as more manuscripts are uncovered, more transcriptions are completed, and more recordings from the period are released or re-released and made accessible, musicological interest in this body of music has surged, led by Gunther Schuller's monumental *The Swing Era: The Development of Jazz, 1930–1945*, volume two of his *History of Jazz*. Schuller's book offers more than 900 pages of description and insight into the stylistic development and influence of dozens of swing bands, complete with analyses of score passages. Yet a book so broad in scope can provide only so much depth on any one musician. More recently, authors have concentrated on comparative studies of the music of a few composers and arrangers, and even on the music of specific individuals.[18] By focusing on Mary Lou

14. Mary Lou Williams, Interview by John S. Wilson, 60.

15. Williams's secular (big band and/or combo) music has been recorded by the Mary Lou Williams Collective (with Geri Allen), the Dutch Jazz Orchestra, the United States Army Field Band/Jazz Ambassadors, and Dave Douglas. Her big band music has been presented in concert by The Smithsonian Jazz Masterworks Orchestra (in New York and Washington, D.C.) and the Lincoln Center Jazz Orchestra (in Alice Tully Hall), including 2010 centenary celebrations by both orchestras. Additional concert performances have been presented by the American Jazz Orchestra, the Carnegie Hall Jazz Orchestra, the North Carolina Jazz Repertory Orchestra, and numerous college and conservatory jazz ensembles. Her music was choreographed in tribute concerts performed by the Contemporary Dance Theater in the late 1980s. A documentary produced by Carol Bash titled *Mary Lou Williams: The Lady Who Swings the Band* is in production and, when completed, will complement the 1990 documentary film *Mary Lou Williams: Music on My Mind*, also about Williams. Since 1996, an annual jazz festival at the John F. Kennedy Center for the Performing Arts has been held in her name. Finally, Williams was the subject of an exhibit titled *Mary Lou Williams: In Her Own Right*, which appeared at Flushing Town Hall in New York in October of 2000.

16. For examples of some of the research that has been done on Williams's music, see Pickeral, "The Masses of Mary Lou Williams"; Kernodle, "Anything You Are Shows Up in Your Music: Mary Lou Williams and the Sanctification of Jazz"; Thompson, "Mary Lou Williams: Zodiac Suite; A Critical Analysis." A book chapter by Hairston, assessing Williams and other female jazz musicians who performed at New York's Café Society, is titled "Gender, Jazz, and the Popular Front." In 2002, the first-ever scholarly conference devoted to Mary Lou Williams was held at the Institute of Jazz Studies at Rutgers University-Newark in New Jersey. A second conference held at the University of Wisconsin-Madison, titled "Symposium: Reflecting on Mary Lou Williams, Envisioning the Future of Jazz," was a part of a Mary Lou Williams Centennial Celebration held in 2010.

17. Recent works of this type (not an exhaustive list) include books like Waters, *The Studio Recordings of the Miles Davis Quintet*; Larson, *Analyzing Jazz*; Givan, "Django Reinhardt's Style and Improvisational Process"; and Martin, *Charlie Parker and Thematic Improvisation*. Many articles in journals such as *Annual Review of Jazz Studies*, *Journal of Jazz Studies*, *Journal of the American Musicological Society*, and *Music Theory Spectrum* also take an analytical approach to solo improvisation.

18. For examples of this sort of work, see van de Leur, *Something to Live For: The Music of Billy Strayhorn*; Mark Tucker, *Ellington*; Magee, *The Uncrowned King of Swing: Fletcher Henderson and Big*

Williams's compositions and arrangements for big band, the work in this volume seeks to begin filling the void of research on this significant part of Williams's career.

FROM PITTSBURGH TO KANSAS CITY

Born in Atlanta, Georgia, in 1910, Mary Lou Williams (born Mary Elfrieda Scruggs) spent most of her youth in Pittsburgh, Pennsylvania, and was quickly recognized as a prodigy at the keyboard. Her mother played the pump organ at a local church, and was shocked one day to hear her three- or four-year-old daughter, seated on her lap, reproduce note-for-note the music she herself had just played. As a child, Williams's musical education was self-directed, but with the support of adults in her life who recognized her burgeoning talent and interest.[19] Her stepfather, Fletcher Burley, bought her a player piano with piano rolls of Jelly Roll Morton and James P. Johnson, and she learned their music by memorizing and duplicating the movement of the piano keys from these rolls. She had perfect pitch and an advanced ear that allowed her to learn and play pieces that she heard on record or in live settings. Williams's talent matured, and by age six she had become known as the "little piano girl," playing for parties and teas throughout the city, including private functions held at the home of the Mellon family, one of the wealthiest and most influential in Pittsburgh.[20] Soon the money she was bringing home significantly bolstered the family's finances.[21] Pittsburgh had a thriving musical scene and served as a destination for many of the traveling musical groups of the day. She would later cite three pianists as particularly influential: Lovie Austin, Pittsburgh native Earl Hines, and another local pianist named Jack Howard, who played in a boogie-woogie style and from whom she learned to play with strength. "He told me always to play the left hand louder than the right because that's where the beat and the feeling was. It's just like a drum keeping a steady beat."[22] Austin accompanied a show on the black vaudeville circuit, and from the time Williams first saw her at work, she aspired to emulate Austin, who could play the show's score with one hand while writing the next act's music with the other, while she conducted and gave musical cues with her head and smoked a cigarette.[23]

Williams first experienced life on the road as a member of Buzzin' Harris's Hits and Bits musical troupe when she was twelve, and although this experience was limited to eight weeks, two years later she was back on the road again, traveling with the same

---

Band Jazz, "The Music of Fletcher Henderson and His Orchestra in the 1920s," and "Before Louis: When Fletcher Henderson was the 'Paul Whiteman of the Race' "; Rattenbury, *Duke Ellington: Jazz Composer*; Howland, *Ellington Uptown: Duke Ellington, James P. Johnson, and the Birth of Concert Jazz*, "Between the Muses and the Masses: Symphonic Jazz, 'Glorified' Entertainment, and the Rise of the American Musical Middlebrow, 1920–1944 (Duke Ellington, James P. Johnson, Paul Whiteman)," and "The Whitemanesque Roots of Early Ellingtonian 'Extended Jazz Composition' "; Chevan, "Written Music in Early Jazz."

19. Kernodle notes the unusual care and support Williams received from family and friends—especially the adult male figures in her life—during her formative years, atypical for the time because of the ways in which women's roles in public entertainment were viewed by society. See *Soul on Soul*, 26.

20. The Mellon family's prominence began with Judge Thomas Mellon (1813–1908), who was born in Ireland but moved to Westmoreland County, Pennsylvania, in 1818. His wealth accumulated through a successful law practice but also through investments in industrial ventures around Pittsburgh, including Andrew Carnegie's growing iron and steel businesses. His two youngest sons, Andrew (1855–1937) and Richard (1858–1933), continued to build upon their father's banking and industrial successes while also becoming philanthropists, founding the National Gallery of Art in Washington, D.C., and providing generous support to libraries and institutions of higher education in and around Pittsburgh. See Ingham, *Biographical Dictionary*, 917–23.

21. Dahl, *Morning Glory*, 23.

22. Mary Lou Williams, Interview by John S. Wilson, 13.

23. Mary Lou Williams, "Autobiography," 88. Written with the help of Max Jones, this article first appeared in several monthly installments in the British magazine *Melody Maker* during 1954.

group again, now on the TOBA (Theater Owners' Booking Agency) black vaudeville circuit. This act folded in 1925, but Williams caught on as the pianist with a popular dance team called Seymour and Jeanette. Her first recordings date from this period, though her first solo recording was not made until 1929.[24] In 1926, the troupe disbanded and she moved with the group's saxophone player, John Williams, to Memphis, where they were married and started a new group called the Syncopators. A short time later, while his new wife stayed in Memphis to keep the Syncopators alive, John Williams accepted a job with the Clouds of Joy, a band based in Oklahoma City, at a salary that promised a brighter future for the young couple. The Clouds of Joy had formed in 1926 in Dallas, Texas. Led originally by trumpeter Terrence Holder, the group carried the name Terrence Holder and the Dark Clouds of Joy, a ten-piece ensemble that played mostly arrangements worked out by ear and remembered by rote (i.e., head arrangements, as opposed to written-out ones). Andy Kirk joined as the group's tuba player in 1927. A territory band signed by Northeast Amusement Company, they relocated in Oklahoma shortly after their formation, playing steady engagements at dance halls in Tulsa and Oklahoma City for nearly three years. In 1929, however, a habit of siphoning the band's money for personal use caught up with Holder. He was forced out, and Kirk (as the band's oldest and most responsible member) was voted in as leader.[25] Meanwhile, Williams found that being an independent seventeen-year-old woman of color in the South at that time could be perilous. By 1928 the Syncopators folded, and she rejoined her husband, traveling with the Clouds of Joy as an unemployed spouse. Despite attempts to convince the members otherwise, Williams was not given a role in the band until a year later, after the band had reorganized and relocated in Kansas City.

By the late 1920s, Kansas City, Missouri, had established itself as a hub in the southwestern United States and, with the aid of a local government that not only tolerated but promoted gambling, prostitution, and illegal distribution of alcohol (in spite of Prohibition), developed an active night life. Some estimates place the number of bars and nightclubs in 1920s Kansas City as high as 500. Under Democratic party boss Tom Pendergast's regime, these businesses thrived and were largely insulated from the effects of the Great Depression that gripped most of the nation in the early 1930s. Music was needed to fill these nightspots and attract customers, and the city became an important center for the development of jazz and blues. Extended an offer to perform at the Pla-Mor Ballroom, one of the city's largest and most popular dance halls, Kirk and the Clouds of Joy went to Kansas City and, after being held over several times, made it their home base.[26] Kansas City also served as the crucible for other, better-known bands such as those led by Bennie Moten, Walter Page, and Count Basie.

Williams made her mark on the group quickly. Under Kirk, she was named as the band's pianist and chief arranger, a dual post she held from 1929 until 1942. Although these roles were unofficial until 1931, Williams can be heard on every one of the band's recordings as pianist and arranger from the time she began traveling with them in 1929. During this time, she produced the vast majority of arrangements in the band's book, composing original songs and arranging pre-existing tunes that crossed boundaries from the smooth, sweet style that Kirk would come increasingly to prefer, to the

24. Williams's first recordings were made with Jeanette's Synco Jazzers in Chicago, sometime in January of 1927. Two sides were cut that day, *Midnight Stomp* (Paramount 12470) and *The Bumps* (Paramount 12451). Both can be heard on Classics 630 (CD).

25. Under Kirk's leadership, the band won success through the 1930s and into the 1940s (corresponding to popularity of swing music in America). The Clouds of Joy disbanded in 1949.

26. The Pla-Mor Ballroom opened in 1927. The three dance halls—Pla-Mor, El Torreon Ballroom, and Paseo Hall—provided nightly opportunities for dancing and became competitors for the top bands to perform. See Driggs and Haddix, *Kansas City Jazz*, 84–87.

Theodore E. Buehrer

hotter, swinging style that appealed most to Williams. Many of the original compositions belong to the latter category. Her reputation as an emerging composer and arranger was noticed, and by the late 1930s and into the 1940s, even and especially after she left the Clouds of Joy, she was providing arrangements for a number of bandleaders, among them Duke Ellington, Benny Goodman, Jimmie Lunceford, Louis Armstrong, Earl Hines, and Tommy Dorsey.

WILLIAMS'S STYLISTIC DEVELOPMENT

After the 1940s, events conspired to lead Williams to stop writing for big band, not returning to that genre until two decades later. Thus, her compositional and arranging efforts for big band encompassed three distinct phases: her first attempts in 1929–31, her polished works from the mid- to late-1930s and the 1940s (though works she created between 1931 and 1936 went unrecorded), and her brief return to the big band after years away from it, in the late 1960s. This study tracks Williams's stylistic evolution and her development as a composer-arranger across all three phases. How did this talented, ambitious young woman who in 1928 could neither read nor notate music become an arranger in such high demand by the late 1930s that she is said to have spent nearly every waking hour writing, even, when necessary, by flashlight in the back of a car as the band traveled by night to the next job? (Williams once reflected, "I was writing for some half-dozen bands each week. As we were making perhaps 500 miles per night, I used to write in the car by flashlight between engagements."[27]) Who influenced Williams, and to what extent? How do those influences manifest themselves in her music? What musical traits define her compositional and arranging style? Cast in the model of other recent works investigating pre-bebop (i.e., written) jazz from a musicological perspective, this study seeks to do more than merely add Williams to the rank of the "exceptional woman." Rather, it seeks to identify her influences, to demonstrate the originality with which she integrated these influences in her music, and to describe the trajectory of her stylistic evolution. Other scholars have done much to heighten awareness of Williams's successful career, but her unique talents as a composer-arranger deserve more recognition than they have so far received.

Williams's style is not easy to define. Ellington's phrase "perpetually contemporary" pointed to a style that was always evolving. As she told Whitney Balliett, "No one can put a style on me. I've learned from many people. I change all the time. I experiment to keep up with what is going on, to hear what everybody else is doing. I even keep a little ahead of them, like a mirror that shows what will happen next."[28] Beyond that, during her tenure with the Clouds of Joy, Williams's style is difficult to pinpoint because of the disparate types of arrangements—from "hot" to "sweet"—she provided for the band. The aesthetic disagreement between Kirk, the band's leader, and Williams, the band's chief composer-arranger and, by the late 1930s, arguably its biggest star, stemmed in part from tastes he acquired during formative years spent in the George Morrison Orchestra, a band that played mostly white society dances in the "sweet" style. But it also reflected Kirk's belief that this style held wide appeal among audiences and that this appeal would boost the group's commercial success. At the same time, it stemmed from his desire, as he put it, "to try to crack the race barrier in recordings."[29] Kirk realized that playing music in the sweeter style challenged stereotypes inherent in the race record industry, which held that black bands should only record hotter, swinging jazz. During the early 1930s, however, the Clouds of Joy began to win popularity

---

27. Mary Lou Williams, "Autobiography," 107.
28. Balliett, "Out Here Again," 53.
29. Kirk and Lee, *Twenty Years on Wheels*, 84.

among black and white audiences, and Kirk wanted to record a more diverse repertoire to reflect the band's widespread appeal.[30] Kirk was a musician but he was also a businessman vying for audiences in a crowded marketplace of competing bands. It is understandable why he would search for whatever angle would bring his band a wider listenership. At the same time, Williams was a valuable asset to the band's success. Over time, Kirk's increasing focus on commercial success through sweeter arrangements and his declining interest in Williams's original compositions in a harder, swinging style contributed to her departure from the band in 1942.[31] Ironically, as the Clouds of Joy achieved greater success, Williams's displeasure grew: "I began to lose interest in the project . . . Sometimes I sat on the stand working crossword puzzles, only playing with my left hand. Every place we played had to turn people away, and my fans must have been disappointed with my conduct. If they were, I wasn't bothering at the time."[32] Peter O'Brien, S.J., Williams's personal assistant and manager in later years, has stated that Williams "did not set the style for Andy Kirk. She set the style only for the majority of the 25 pieces or so that are constantly reissued" from that period.[33] While she arranged some of the Kirk band's "sweet" charts, she was not responsible for all of them, and the ones she did arrange reflect a professional's ability to turn out work addressed to the marketplace her employer sought to serve. The "25 pieces or so" mentioned by O'Brien refer to Williams's "hot" contributions to the band's library, most of them originals. They are the best indicators of how Williams's personal style evolved. It is this body of work, together with the compositions and arrangements written for other bandleaders in the 1930s and 1940s and the handful of arrangements produced in 1967–68, from which examples are drawn throughout this study.

Williams and the Clouds of Joy: 1929–31

The thriving musical scene in Williams's hometown of Pittsburgh gave her ample exposure to the music she would make her life's work from the time she was a child. But not until years later, as a member of the Clouds of Joy, did she learn to read and write music. Her first arranging efforts were rough, occurring shortly after Kirk's band relocated to Kansas City. Of these attempts, Williams recalled that

> [I]n Kansas City, Kirk had liked my ideas, though I could not set them down on paper. He would sit up as long as twelve hours at a stretch, taking down my ideas for arrangements, and I got so sick of the method that I began putting them down myself. I hadn't studied theory, but asked Kirk about chords and the voicing register. In about 15 minutes I had memorized what I wanted. That's how I started writing. My first attempt, "Messa Stomp," was beyond the range of half the instruments.[34]

---

30. See also Kernodle, *Soul on Soul*, 69.

31. To suggest that Kirk's and Williams's different stylistic preferences caused her to leave the band in 1942, however, fails to present a complete picture. Peter O'Brien confirms that, while Williams once told him that Kirk's band sometimes sounded "like Guy Lombardo," she made her comment without malice or dislike, but simply as a statement of fact (Peter O'Brien, private communication, 2003). Indeed, Williams and Kirk were fond of each other, and her reasons for leaving the band in 1942 were multifaceted, reaching beyond the scope of this essay.

32. Mary Lou Williams, "Autobiography," 107.

33. Dahl, *Morning Glory*, 98. O'Brien first met Williams in 1964 and began representing her in an unofficial capacity two years later. By 1970, and until her death in 1981, O'Brien was Williams's close friend and personal manager. Today he serves as the Executive Director of the Mary Lou Williams Foundation, Mary Records, and the Cecilia Music Publishing Company. He promotes Williams's musical legacy by overseeing recording projects and reissues, speaking at festivals and events featuring her music, and touting the Mary Lou Williams Collection housed at the Institute of Jazz Studies (University of Rutgers-Newark, Newark, NJ).

34. Mary Lou Williams, "Autobiography," 98.

Theodore E. Buehrer

Table 1.   Mary Lou Williams's compositions for Kirk's Clouds of Joy, 1929–31

Title	Recording Date	Location	Matrix	Original Recording	CD Reissue	Basic Form
Mess-a-Stomp	11/7/29	Kansas City	KC-591-A	Brunswick 4694	Classics 655	Blues
*Cloudy**	11/7/29	Kansas City	KC-593-A	Brunswick 4653	Classics 655	Blues
Lotta Sax Appeal†	11/9/29	Kansas City	KC-601-A	Vocalion 1453	Classics 655	Blues/*aaba*
*Corky Stomp**	11/11/29	Kansas City	KC-618-A	Brunswick 4893	Classics 655	*abab'*
Froggy Bottom	11/11/29	Kansas City	KC-619-A	Brunswick 4893	Classics 655	Blues
*Loose Ankles**	4/29/30	Chicago	C-4462-A	Brunswick 4803	Classics 655	*aaba*
Mary's Idea	4/30/30	Chicago	C-4473-	Brunswick 4863	Classics 655	*aaba*
Gettin' off a Mess‡	7/15/30	Chicago	C-6017-	Brunswick 7180	Classics 655	*aba* (8+8+8)

*Some sources give co-composer credit to Andy Kirk. The arrangement, however, is most likely Williams's.

†Some sources give co-composer credit to Mary Lou Williams's husband, John Williams. The arrangement itself, however, is Mary Lou Williams's.

‡*Gettin' off a Mess* was recorded by a group called the Seven Little Clouds of Joy, a septet drawn from the larger group.

In a 1973 interview, reflecting more generally on her early arranging efforts, Williams is kinder to herself, saying that only the balance between tenor sax and trombone needed adjustment in those first arrangements.[35] On another occasion she reflected on the support and encouragement her bandmates had offered her, even at this early stage: "The boys gave me a chance and each time I did better."[36] But Williams held herself to high standards, and expected the same from the musicians in the band: "When the boys fooled around at rehearsals with what I wrote, I got mad and snatched the music off their stands and began to cry and went home to bed."[37] Clearly she was a quick study, because Kirk's band recorded eight tunes at its first session for Brunswick in November of 1929 (at radio station KMBC in Kansas City), and "five of them [were] written by Mary or originating with her."[38] Table 1 shows Williams's compositions for Kirk from 1929 to 1931.

Listening to and absorbing the musical sounds she heard had always been a source of learning and inspiration for Williams, and her development of that awareness continued during her early years with the Clouds of Joy. Kirk verified this fact, saying, "She would have certain chords in her mind but she didn't at first know how to voice them . . . If she wasn't out all night at the jazz clubs in Kansas City, listening and getting ideas, she'd be sitting up at the foot of the bed, legs crossed like an Indian, just writing and writing"[39] (meaning that, rather than inventing music at the piano, Williams preferred to work out musical ideas in her head). Among bands that Williams would surely have heard during her late-night listening sessions were McKinney's Cotton Pickers, whose musical director at the time was Don Redman, and the Casa Loma Orchestra, whose style was forged by arranger Gene Gifford. Though

35. Mary Lou Williams, Interview by John S. Wilson, 47–48.
36. Mary Lou Williams, "Autobiography," 98.
37. Wilson, "Mary Lou Williams: A Jazz Great, Dies," section 1, page 21, column 1.
38. Dahl, *Morning Glory*, 74. The remaining three tunes arranged but not composed by Williams that were recorded during the band's first recording session were *Blue Clarinet Stomp*, *Casey Jones Special*, and *Somepin' Slow and Low*.
39. Kirk and Lee, *Twenty Years on Wheels*, 73.

the Cotton Pickers did not travel west through Kansas City until early 1931, Williams probably heard them when the Clouds of Joy traveled east to New York for the first time in January of 1930.[40] The Clouds spent six weeks at the Roseland Ballroom during their first New York visit, playing for two of those weeks opposite the Casa Loma Orchestra.[41] Williams cites both Redman and Gifford as important early influences.

But listening was not Williams's only form of study. Early in 1930 (likely during the New York trip) Kirk purchased approximately 40 arrangements for his band from Hank Biagini of the Orange Blossoms (later the Casa Loma Orchestra).[42] Some of these were by Redman, others by Gifford. Kirk indicates that Williams studied and learned from this cache of written music: "As time went on she learned voicing for the different horns from things I showed her from some arrangements I'd bought."[43] The band may have acquired more new material during its engagement at the Savoy Ballroom, which followed their stay at the Roseland.[44] The impact of this new music was enough to convince Kirk that "we sounded like a new band."[45] And it provided Williams with more resources to study. Williams's biographer Linda Dahl stresses the importance of these arrangements, asserting that Kirk encouraged Williams to tailor them for the Clouds of Joy and its players' particular strengths.[46]

Thus, in a city with as much music as Kansas City at this time, Williams absorbed the style characteristics that were crystallizing there and that would become earmarks of jazz music emanating from the Southwest: a relaxed yet hard-driving, four-beat swing feel; heavy emphasis on the blues form and melodies built on the blues scale; and ample room for extended individual improvisation with riff-based backgrounds that were frequently worked out by ear and learned aurally. In 1930, Kirk's band consisted of three reeds (one tenor and two altos, one of which doubled on clarinet, the other on baritone), three brass (two trumpets and a trombone), and a rhythm section of piano, banjo, tuba, and drums. This instrumentation was considered normal for Kansas City bands at the time. Yet Williams's developing musical aesthetic was also informed by other music she heard from the so-called "East Coast" swing bands. Her use of *aaba* song form (as opposed to the blues), tightly voiced harmonizations of melodies, chord vocabulary, and keen sense of dramatic timing and build are all on display in her early-1930s arrangements. They reveal an understanding of the practices pioneered by arrangers like Redman, Gifford, and other East Coast-based musicians. Thus, in Williams's hands, the band's identity—yet to be firmly established—was still emerging, it seems, from a part of her musical consciousness that was seeking to reconcile the eastern and the Kansas City styles.

Williams's influences reveal themselves in various guises in her early arrangements. Proving her comment that "Redman was my model," there are several instances in which an idea that appears in a Don Redman arrangement shows up plainly in one of

---

40. Chilton, *McKinney's Music*, 34.

41. Kirk and Lee, *Twenty Years on Wheels*, 72.

42. There is some confusion about the chronology, but the Orange Blossoms were renamed the Casa Loma Orchestra around 1929. Kirk refers to them by both names, even though they were the same band.

43. Kirk and Lee, *Twenty Years on Wheels*, 73.

44. At the Savoy, the Clouds of Joy played opposite Chick Webb's band. Williams biographer Linda Dahl states that during this time Webb's group included saxophonist and arranger Benny Carter, asserting that Carter supplied John Williams with copies of some of Webb's current arrangements for five dollars apiece, among them *Ol' Man River* and *Liza* (see Dahl, *Morning Glory*, 80). The timing of this supposed transaction is suspect, however, as Carter did not join Webb's band until March of 1931, and left in August for McKinney's Cotton Pickers. See Berger, Berger, and Patrick, *Benny Carter*. It could be that Dahl's information, gathered during an interview with John Williams, is based on Williams's faulty memory for dates, and that Carter supplied these charts during the Clouds' next East Coast trip, which lasted from December 1930 into the spring of 1931. On the other hand, neither Andy Kirk nor Mary Lou Williams ever mentioned receiving these arrangements from Webb by way of Carter.

45. Kirk and Lee, *Twenty Years on Wheels*, 73.

46. Dahl, *Morning Glory*, 80.

Theodore E. Buehrer

Williams's scores.[47] Direct influence of this kind can be observed by comparing the introductions to Redman's *Cotton Picker's Scat* and *Hullabaloo*, both recorded in 1930, to Williams's introduction to *Mary's Idea*, recorded the same year.[48] It is reasonable to assume that Williams heard the Cotton Pickers play these tunes. As staples of that band's book, both would have been played frequently. Reduced score passages of these introductions appear as Examples 1a–c.[49] The deep similarity in voicing (mostly close spacing of triadic harmonies) and especially in rhythm (the short-long, eighth-note/dotted quarter-note motive that recurs in each example) are clear. Yet Williams's introduction to *Mary's Idea* does more than just copy and recycle Redman's ideas. Her introduction is roughly twice as long as either of Redman's, and while her saxophones remain tightly spaced throughout, she opens up her brass voicings considerably after the opening phrase. Thus, while the sources of her inspiration are obvious, it is equally so that she extends and modifies Redman's model as she finds appropriate.

A second example of direct influence, though harder to hear, is cited by Max Harrison as well as Williams's biographer Linda Dahl. A comparison of Williams's arrangement of *Travelin' that Rocky Road*, recorded in October of 1930, to Redman's *Rocky Road*, from November of the same year, brings the influence to light.[50] Much about these two arrangements differs, including a vocal chorus in Redman's version that is lacking in Williams's purely instrumental arrangement. Nevertheless, Harrison finds in Williams's arrangement "an obvious Redman influence, the opening saxophone chorus being a spin-off from the McKinney's version." Examples 2a and 2b provide excerpts from the two arrangements for side-by-side comparison, which shows a certain similarity of rhythmic motive and melodic shape. The differences, however, reveal Williams's independence of mind. Redman's chorus is for the full ensemble, contains call and response between brass and reeds, and comes at the end of the arrangement. Williams's chorus, for saxophone soli, begins the arrangement and is only loosely based on Redman's brass line. This example, along with the one previously cited, not to mention others, shows Williams's sure sense, even early in her arranging career, of what to borrow and how to use it to better her own work.

Williams's early arrangements and compositions show both examples of direct influence and moments in which the influence is harder to identify. Biographer Tammy Kernodle notes that Williams's style "had been groomed in the blues she heard as a young child, the vaudeville shows of the TOBA, and the jazz sessions and nightlife of Kansas City," and that her earliest arrangements demonstrate attempts "to fuse these idioms into the 'sweet' band rhythms and harmonies that had defined Kirk's sound until this point."[51] Such influences may be seen by examining other musical parameters, including form, harmony, voicing, texture, and the balance between written and improvised passages. A glance at Table 1, for example, reveals that Williams was not beholden to blues forms despite their overwhelming prevalence on the Kansas City music scene. She implements other song forms, such as *aaba*, and *abab* structures whose origins lie more in vaudeville and Tin Pan Alley. To gain a more accurate picture of the proportion of blues and alternate song forms in the Clouds of Joy book during this period, it is worth noting that of the twenty-four sides they recorded from 1929 to

47. Balliett, "Out Here Again," 61.

48. There is no known surviving score of the 1930 version of *Mary's Idea*. The score excerpts that appear in this essay and the edition that appears in this volume are my own transcriptions. The Clouds of Joy recorded the arrangement on 1 May 1930.

49. All music examples presented here are my own transcriptions and differ from transcriptions by Mark Lopeman, which exist in the Mary Lou Williams Collection. In the examples instruments are transposed to sounding pitch.

50. Harrison, "Swing Era Big Bands," 287. Dahl refers to the same two pieces to document Redman's influence on Williams (see *Morning Glory*, 78). A reissue of Williams's arrangement is found on Classics 655 (CD); Redman's arrangement (also reissued) can be heard on Frog DGF 25.

51. Kernodle, *Soul on Soul*, 58–59.

Example 1a. Redman, *Cotton Picker's Scat*, introduction (mm. 1–4)

Example 1b. Redman, *Hullabaloo*, introduction (mm. 1–6)

Example 1c. Williams, *Mary's Idea* (1930), introduction (mm. 1–10)

Example 2a.   Redman, *Rocky Road*, mm. 73–80 (1st *a* section of final chorus)

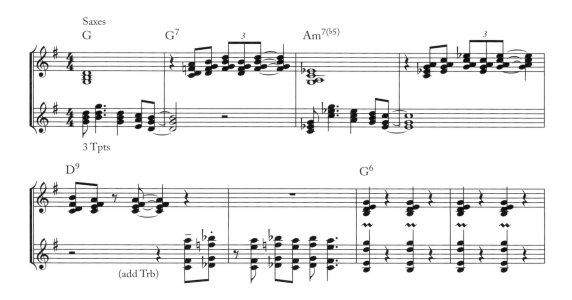

Example 2b.   Williams, *Travelin' that Rocky Road*, mm. 17–24 (2nd *a* section of first chorus)

1931 (most of them arranged by Williams), almost two-thirds (fifteen of twenty-four) exhibit non-blues forms of one sort or another.

The 1930 version of *Mary's Idea*, included in this edition, is a good example of Williams's use of a popular song form. Following the introduction, *Mary's Idea* unfolds as a thirty-two-bar *aaba* tune (Form Diagram 1). The band plays four choruses, with an extended interlude based on material from the *a* section inserted between the second and third choruses. During this early period Williams's arrangements frequently went beyond a single formal model. Interludes were common in big band music of the day, especially in arrangements with vocalists whose voice range called for a modulation. But in other instances Williams juxtaposed two or more formal structures in the same arrangement. For example, Table 1 classifies *Mess-a-Stomp* as a blues, and for much of the arrangement, which is transcribed in this edition, the repetitive twelve-bar blues progression is easily followed (Form Diagram 2). But in the middle (X, B1, B2 in the diagram) Williams inserts a four-measure transition plus a repeated eight-measure strain consisting of a saxophone soli and a trumpet solo. Both the sax soli and trumpet solo vamp on two chords, Gm and D7, before the arrangement returns to twelve-bar sections, of which the first two (C) deviate from the blues progression and

Form Diagram 1. *Mary's Idea* (1930)

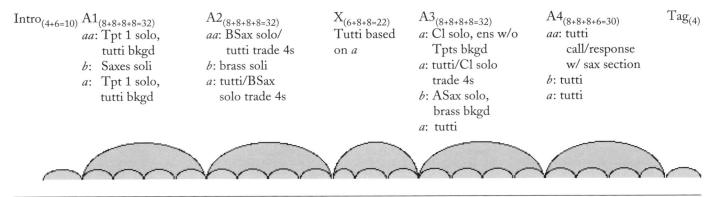

Intro$_{(4+6=10)}$ A1$_{(8+8+8+8=32)}$ A2$_{(8+8+8+8=32)}$ X$_{(6+8+8=22)}$ A3$_{(8+8+8=32)}$ A4$_{(8+8+8+6=30)}$ Tag$_{(4)}$

    aa: Tpt 1 solo,   *aa*: BSax solo/   Tutti based   *a*: Cl solo, ens w/o   *aa*: tutti

       tutti bkgd   tutti trade 4s   on *a*   Tpts bkgd   call/response

    b: Saxes soli   *b*:   brass soli   *a*: tutti/Cl solo   w/ sax section

    a: Tpt 1 solo,   *a*:   tutti/BSax   trade 4s   *b*: tutti

       tutti bkgd   solo trade 4s   *b*: ASax solo,   *a*: tutti

                                         brass bkgd

                                     a: tutti

Abbreviations.   bkgd = background; ens = ensemble; trade 4s = 4 measure trading; w/o = without; w/ = with.

Form Diagram 2. *Mess–a–Stomp* (1929)

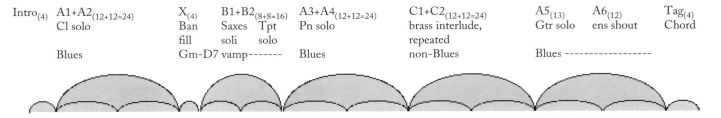

Intro$_{(4)}$ A1+A2$_{(12+12=24)}$ X$_{(4)}$ B1+B2$_{(8+8=16)}$ A3+A4$_{(12+12=24)}$ C1+C2$_{(12+12=24)}$ A5$_{(13)}$ A6$_{(12)}$ Tag$_{(4)}$

       Cl solo   Ban   Saxes   Tpt   Pn solo   brass interlude,   Gtr solo   ens shout   Chord

               fill   soli   solo   repeated

       Blues   Gm-D7 vamp-------   Blues   non-Blues   Blues ------------------

the last two (A3 and A4) reaffirm it. *Lotta Sax Appeal*, among the other tunes recorded at this November 1929 session, presents an even more varied formal structure (Form Diagram 3). Following an eight-measure introduction, it presents two choruses of blues as a vehicle for a baritone saxophone solo. Two sixteen-bar non-blues strains follow, as the baritone sax trades two-measure phrases with the brass before the blues progression returns for a two-chorus trombone solo. Finally, the arrangement closes with two thirty-two-bar choruses in *aaba* format that include ensemble tutti passages as well as eight- and sixteen-bar passages for piano, baritone saxophone, trumpet, and collective ensemble improvisation. The opening melody of *Corky Stomp*, also from the same session, exhibits an *abab'* structure and a major key, but this form is not applied consistently throughout the arrangement (Form Diagram 4). The head is followed by two eight-measure strains in minor, the first for saxophone soli, the second for trumpet solo. These strains give way to a thirty-two-bar piano solo exhibiting *aaba* form, before the *ab'* passage from the opening head reappears to end the performance. In what could be considered Williams's most adventurous experiment with formal structure during this period, *Gettin' off a Mess*, recorded in July of 1930 by a combo called the Seven Little Clouds of Joy, employs a twenty-four-bar structure in *aba* form (Form Diagram 5). This tune, primarily a head arrangement that serves as a vehicle for multiple improvisations, follows this *aba* structure for four choruses. Between the second and third chorus, Williams inserts a fourteen-bar interlude that modulates to the dominant, and a repeated eight-measure strain in the new key, both involving written-out parts for the full ensemble.

Another aspect of Williams's adaptation of conventional formal structures is her treatment of phrase length, as seen in the introduction and the interlude of *Mary's Idea*. Whereas conventional phrase lengths tend toward groupings in fours and eights, the introduction to *Mary's Idea* is ten measures long, comprising a four-bar phrase followed

                                 Theodore E. Buehrer

Form Diagram 3.   *Lotta Sax Appeal* (1929)

Intro$_{(8)}$ A1+A2$_{(12+12=24)}$ B1+B2$_{(16+16=32)}$ A3+A4$_{(12+12=24)}$ C1$_{(32)}$ C2$_{(32)}$
            BSax solo   BSax solo/brass   Trb solo   *aa*: ens   *aa*: BSax solo
                                   trade 2s   *b*: Pn solo   *b*: Tpt solo
                                                                                 a: ens   *a*: ens improv
            Blues   16-bar strain, repeated   Blues   *aaba*   *aaba*

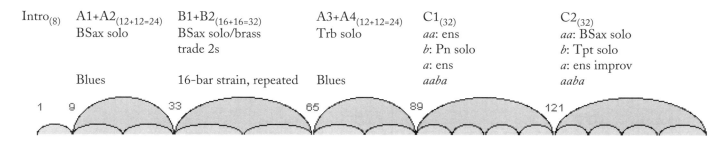

Form Diagram 4.   *Corky Stomp* (1929)

Intro$_{(3+3=6)}$ A1$_{(32)}$ B1$_{(8+8=16)}$ C$_{(32)}$ A2$_{(8+6=14)}$ Tag$_{(4)}$
            Trb solo melody   1x: Sax soli   Pn solo   Sax soli w/
            w/ Tpt bkgd   2x: Tpt solo   brass improv
            abab'   *cc'*   *aada*   *ab'*

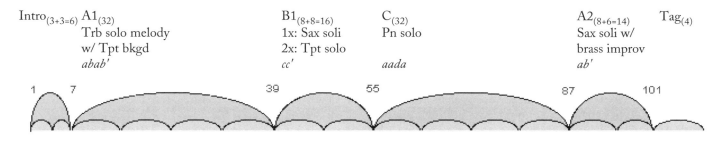

Form Diagram 5.   *Gettin' off a Mess* (1930)

Intro$_{(4)}$ A1$_{(8+8+8=24)}$ A2$_{(8+(8+6)=22)}$ X$_{(4+4+6=14)}$ B$_{(8+8=16)}$ A3$_{(8+8+8=24)}$ A4$_{(8+8+8=24)}$
            Sax solo chorus   Trb solo   Pn solo   whole tone/   ens strain   Tpt solo chorus   ens chorus
                                                         modulatory   (repeated)
                                                         interlude
            aba   *a --------- ba*   *xyz*   *cc*   *aba*   *aba*

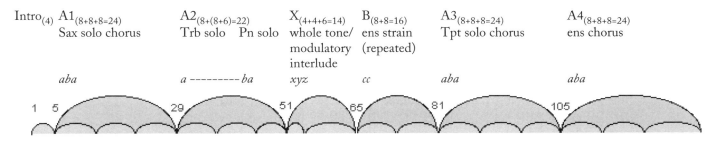

by a six-bar one. Likewise, the interlude (twenty-two measures) begins with a six-bar phrase, followed by two eight-bar statements. Williams's free treatment of phrase lengths is evident through this early period, and it remains a characteristic of her later writing as well. The introduction to *Corky Stomp* is six bars long, split into three-bar phrases. As noted, *Gettin' off a Mess* also contains phrases of irregular length.[52]

Harmonically, Williams's compositions from this time feature a palette that would have been comparable to most other arrangers from the period: major, minor, and diminished triads, dominant sevenths and ninths (occasionally with a raised fifth), and added-sixth chords. An added-sixth chord ending can be seen in *Corky Stomp* (Example 3). Interestingly, Williams asserted that she was the first to use the added-sixth chord in jazz, saying,

---

52. Of the tunes mentioned in this section on formal structure, no original scores or parts survive in the Mary Lou Williams Collection.

Example 3.   Williams, excerpt from *Corky Stomp,* tag ending showing added sixth chord (mm. 101–5)

> I discovered chords and Andy used to say to me, "You can't do that. It's against the rules of writing music." I said, "But I hear a sixth in this chord." He said, "But you can't do it" . . . He kept telling me it was against the rules of the chord. In that year I guess it was but . . . I found these things on the piano and I said this will sound good.[53]

Although her claim is inaccurate (the use of added-sixth chords in popular music predates Williams's use of them by several years), the absence of this harmony from the music she heard playing in Kansas City's nightclubs and ballrooms may have convinced her that these chords were her own discovery. Kirk's recollection of his first encounters with Don Redman's arrangements seems to corroborate that the chord was uncommon in Kansas City:

> There were good music kicks right at the Pla-Mor, when bands like McKinney's Cotton Pickers or Fletcher Henderson shared the stand with us. The Cotton Pickers played something I'd never heard before; a sixth in a chord. In some places it sounded to me like a clash. I was used to triads, dominant sevenths, a dominant ninth occasionally, and diminished chords. Later I got to like the sound of the sixth, especially the way Don Redman used it in his arrangements, as a 13th an octave higher.[54]

Whether or not the facts support her claim, the story points to Williams's inclination to explore sounds that were new to her, a predilection that persisted throughout her career.

While triads, dominant sevenths, and added sixth chords were the primary components of Williams's tonal language, a striking diversion from these harmonies occurs in *Gettin' off a Mess.* Here, Williams writes a transition passage that, modulating from the tonic of F major to its dominant, C major, explores the use of whole tones (WT) in two ways (Example 4). In X/1–3, Williams planes major and major-minor 9th chords along the F whole-tone scale, sandwiched between two tonic (F major) triads. The following passage, X/5–8, is derived from the F♯ whole-tone scale, a dramatic harmonic departure from F major and a tritone away from the eventual harmonic goal of the passage, C major. *Gettin' off a Mess* is Williams's only recorded arrangement from this period to use this scale, though she certainly was aware of its harmonic potential. In fact, she explored whole-tone harmonies in her own piano solo work during this time, as in her solo on *Corky Stomp* from 1929. Though such jazz arrangers as Bill Challis, Ferde Grofé, and others who worked for Paul Whiteman experimented with this scale prior to Williams, its use was not commonplace in swing arrangements, and especially not in Kansas City.[55] Williams's use of this scale in her composing and arranging is

53. Mary Lou Williams, Interview by John S. Wilson, 49.
54. Kirk and Lee, *Twenty Years on Wheels,* 66.
55. See Youngren, "European Roots of Jazz," 17–28, for discussion of Challis and Whiteman.

Theodore E. Buehrer

Example 4.   Williams, interlude from *Gettin' off a Mess* (X/1–14 followed by B/1–2, mm. 51–66)

another demonstration of her advanced sense of harmony, her willingness to break away from familiar conventions and influences, and the trust she had in her own compositional instincts to guide her.

In balancing improvised and written passages, whether for full ensemble or sections of the band, Williams's earliest arrangements leaned toward improvisation. Among the five compositions from the November 1929 recording sessions (*Mess-a-Stomp*, *Cloudy*, *Froggy Bottom*, *Corky Stomp*, and *Lotta Sax Appeal*), it is likely that only the introductions, endings, backgrounds for soloists (which were frequent), and occasional tutti passages would have been written out.[56] Otherwise the performance of melodies and call-and-response riffs would have been played from memory. As Williams grew more

---

56. This statement can only be made conjecturally (i.e., "it is likely . . .") because no written sources are extant for these compositions.

familiar with East Coast arrangements, however, her own work began to balance written and improvised passages more equally. Thus, her work began to include more passages composed for the ensemble than did arrangements played by most other Kansas City bands. At the same time, her arrangements offered more improvised solo opportunities than did those of Don Redman or Gene Gifford. Again, *Mary's Idea* makes the point. The music leaves ample room for improvisation, with solo opportunities for trumpet, baritone sax, clarinet, and alto sax. The final shout chorus aside, improvised soloing fills more than half of the piece. Though the East Coast style included room for improvisation, solos tended to be interspersed in short (four- or eight-measure) blocks, and less often extended for as many as sixteen bars, as is the opening trumpet solo here. The heightened emphasis on the soloist also includes frequent trading between soloist and ensemble, another trait aligned more closely with the Kansas City style than with the East Coast approach. The baritone saxophone soloist "trades fours" with the ensemble in the *a* sections of the second chorus, and the clarinet soloist does the same in the second *a* section of the third chorus.[57] Trading between soloists and ensemble also occurs in *Lotta Sax Appeal*, and alternating between two soloists (tuba and clarinet) occurs in *Cloudy*.

During her formative years as a composer and an arranger, Williams used several of the textural combinations available to her: melody and accompaniment, block chords (both examples of homophony), and sectional call and response (i.e., antiphony). But she mixed textures in varying ways, tending to favor particular ones in particular roles. For example, she frequently began numbers (following the introduction) with melody and accompaniment: solo horn playing either the tune's melody (if one existed) or simply improvising over chord changes, often with other instrumental sections providing backgrounds. All of Williams's eight original compositions and several of her arrangements from that time (as the band's chief arranger, she would have arranged the majority of songs that the band performed, even if she had not composed them herself) follow this model (see Form Diagrams 1–5 for a sampling). Obviously, any improvisatory passage featuring a single soloist with other instrumental background belongs to this category as well. Thus, Williams's emphasis on improvised solos in her arrangements gives this texture prominence in her work. Less important, but still frequently used, was block chordal (soli) texture, in which a melody is harmonized with chords sounded by instruments moving in identical rhythms. Williams frequently used the full ensemble to create this texture, but she reserved it for introductions, arrangement-ending shout choruses, and occasional backgrounds for soloists. Individual instrumental sections (reeds or brass) were also used in this way to harmonize a melodic line or to provide background chords or lines behind soloists. She also used other combinations of instruments in her background writing to explore different timbral possibilities. For example, in *Cloudy* she used a trumpet/alto saxophone/trombone trio to harmonize a background line behind a baritone saxophone solo: a sound with an Ellingtonian ring to it. *Mary's Idea* features two unique instrumental combinations: an alto sax/tenor sax/trombone combination supplying background harmonies for a clarinet solo (Form Diagram 1, A3/1–8, 13–16), and a grouping of trumpet, trombone, two alto saxes and one tenor sax providing a harmonized background figure that supports a solo trumpet melody (A1/1–6 and A1/9–15). Less frequent, but worth mentioning as a link to the jazz style that emerged from New Orleans and migrated to Chicago during the 1920s (and was practiced in Kansas City), is Williams's use of collective improvisation (two or more instruments improvising simultaneously) in arrangements from this period.

---

57. "Trading fours" is a common improvisatory technique in jazz whereby two or more musicians take turns improvising four-measure passages as the structure of the composition moves along. In this instance, the procedure is varied slightly, since the baritone saxophonist is taking turns with the rest of the ensemble, and the latter plays pre-arranged (i.e., not improvised) music.

Theodore E. Buehrer

The technique appears in *Cloudy*, *Lotta Sax Appeal*, *Froggy Bottom*, and *Corky Stomp*, all from the November 1929 recording sessions. These instances in the style of collective improvisation always occur at the climax of the arrangements, as Williams pits the improvising instruments (never exceeding three) against the rest of the ensemble, which plays pre-arranged music. Collective improvisation does not appear on the Clouds of Joy recordings after 1929, however. Williams seems to have dropped it as her style and arranging approach evolved. Perhaps it began to sound old-fashioned to her.

The texture least exploited, at least at this stage in Williams's development, is the call-and-response interchange between instrumental sections (reeds and brass): an innovation generally ascribed to Don Redman in the 1920s when he was with the Fletcher Henderson orchestra.[58] This is not to say that Williams never pits reeds against brass in her earliest recordings.[59] But she had not yet fully made this antiphonal technique part of her arranging style. Nevertheless, Redman's influence is evident in the number of instrumental combinations her arrangements employed, as well as the use of block chord voicings behind soloists. And though Williams's work from this period does not emphasize sectional interplay, the full, homogeneous ensemble textures prevalent in her arrangements are characteristic of Gene Gifford's writing for the Casa Loma Orchestra. Though recordings made by the Clouds of Joy exhibit neither the faster tempos nor the level of precision of the Casa Loma group, Williams was clearly drawn to the driving, full ensemble sound that was one of that band's specialties.

Like many bands, the Clouds of Joy fell on hard times in the early 1930s with the onset of the Great Depression. The band's second trip east at the end of 1930 included two recording sessions, the first in New York in December of 1930, and the second with singer Blanche Calloway in Camden, New Jersey, in March of 1931. But following the March session, the group found itself stranded on the East Coast, unable to get back to Kansas City. Finally, in May, the Clouds of Joy landed an engagement in Baltimore that funded their return trip home.

Williams and the Clouds of Joy: 1931–42

Once back in Kansas City, they did not fare much better, even though local politics still insulated Kansas City somewhat from the effects of the Depression. The work they found in the city was insufficient to sustain them, so the Clouds of Joy often went on the road. Kirk writes, "If we weren't on location in Kansas City, we'd go out on one-nighters, following those spokes into known and unknown territory. Playing one-nighters in those Depression years of the early 1930s was all part of making a living in music. We didn't have to depend on one location."[60]

Despite the difficulties of life on the road, the Clouds of Joy prospered musically during this period, which saw significant personnel changes. A comparison of the 1936 group to the 1931 group reveals only six holdovers: Andy Kirk, Mary Lou Williams, John Williams, John Harrington (clarinet/alto saxophone), Harry Lawson (trumpet), and Claude Williams (violin and guitar).[61] Also during this period, the Clouds of Joy

---

58. Maher and Sultanof, "Pre-Swing Era Big Bands and Jazz Composing and Arranging," 270.

59. For example, *Mary's Idea* contains some call and response between sections, as do arrangements of *Snag It*, *Sweet and Hot*, and others.

60. Kirk and Lee, *Twenty Years on Wheels*, 74.

61. The presence of a violinist in a jazz band may seem odd. The violin would not have played a role in the hotter, swing numbers played by the Clouds of Joy (without amplification, it would have been drowned out by the other instruments), but the Clouds, like every band at this time, played nightly in a wide range of styles for dancing, and the violin would have complemented the band's sound in many of

gained the first of a string of gifted tenor saxophone soloists when Ben Webster joined the band in 1932 or 1933. Lester Young replaced Webster after a couple of years, but Young remained only a short time. Buddy Tate followed him, and was in turn succeeded by Dick Wilson in 1936. The band picked up trumpeter Earl Thompson in 1933 or 1934; he also provided some arrangements, lightening Williams's burden as the band's sole arranger. Kirk solidified his rhythm section with the additions of Booker Collins on bass and Ben Thigpen on drums. And they added vocalist Pha Terrell, whose vocal stylings would become a primary reason for the band's commercial success in the late 1930s. From 1931 to 1936, the band grew from ten members (two trumpets, trombone, three reeds, piano, banjo, tuba, drums) to twelve (with Kirk now just conducting, the band consisted of three trumpets, adding Paul King to Lawson and Thompson; two trombones, Ted Donnelly and Henry Wells; three reeds, Harrington, Wilson, and John Williams; piano, Mary Lou Williams; guitar, Ted Brinson; Collins on bass, and Thigpen on drums),[62] even as the trend among big bands was moving toward an even larger instrumentation of six or seven brass and five reeds plus a rhythm section. Despite its larger size, creating more variables and moving pieces, the 1936 ensemble played with greater precision and accuracy and swung more convincingly than the 1929–31 group.

Because the Clouds of Joy went unrecorded from 1931 until 1936 and there are no surviving scores, it is impossible to chronicle Williams's evolution as a composer during that period. Beginning with the band's first recordings from March of 1936, however, her development may be traced. By this time, Williams's compositional and arranging influences had broadened to include Edgar Sampson, chief arranger for Chick Webb, and Eddie Durham, who arranged for Count Basie and before him for Jimmie Lunceford. Her compositions and arrangements for the Clouds of Joy were light and uncluttered, and continued to emphasize improvised solos. It is also true, however, that the band's growing popularity was based largely on its commercially successful vocal arrangements, especially after its hit *Until the Real Thing Comes Along* was recorded in April of 1936. Figures 1a and 1b reveal that the balance between recordings of instrumental and vocal arrangements tipped decidedly in the favor of vocal arrangements in the ensuing years, particularly after Pha Terrell was added to the group.

Nevertheless, Williams's instrumental arrangements suggest a more sophisticated and inventive approach to her work, showing that she had indeed assimilated arranging conventions of the day from Redman, Sampson, Durham, and perhaps others, while continuing to experiment and explore opportunities for innovation. Table 2 lists all of Williams's compositions for Andy Kirk that were recorded between 1936 and 1942 (some of them, already recorded in 1929, were provided with a new arrangement). Tunes such as *Bearcat Shuffle* and *Steppin' Pretty* (1936), *In the Groove* and *A Mellow Bit of Rhythm* (1937), *Dunkin' a Doughnut* (1938), and *Scratchin' in the Gravel* (1940) exhibit a straightforward approach to musical form, harmonic language, and conventional sectional and ensemble writing. Other tunes from this period show Williams stretching conventional boundaries. For example, while *Walkin' and Swingin'* (contained in this edition) sticks to a thirty-two-bar *aaba* format, Williams experiments with instrumental combinations linked to a thicker block chord texture in the saxophone chorus. As she describes, "I needed a fourth saxophone, but during that period you had only three. As I didn't have a fourth, I used a trumpet with a hat—a wah-wah thing—for the eighth notes. This was an innovation for the time; musicians loved

the slower, sweeter styles they played, such as the waltz. Claude Williams, in addition to playing the violin, is also identified as the solo guitarist on *Mess-a-Stomp*, but he is no longer listed among the band's personnel in any capacity after 1937.

62. The Clouds of Joy added another alto saxophonist, Earl Miller, in late 1936 or early 1937, bringing their personnel total to thirteen.

Theodore E. Buehrer

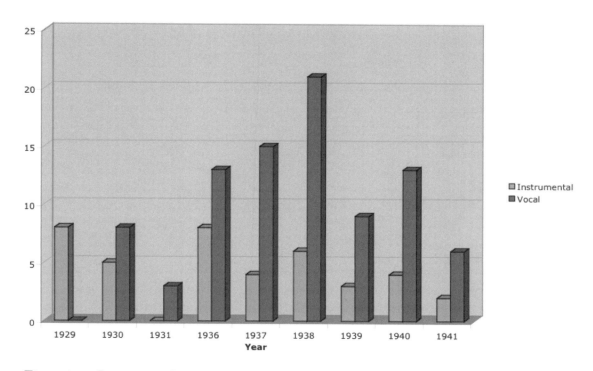

Figure 1a.   Instrumental vs. vocal arrangements, 1929–41

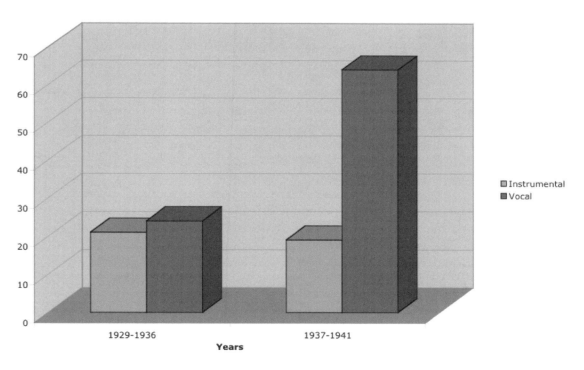

Figure 1b.   Instrumental vs. vocal arrangements, before/after addition of Pha Terrell

Table 2. Mary Lou Williams's compositions for Kirk's Clouds of Joy, 1936–42

Title	Recording Date	Location	Matrix	Original Recording	CD Reissue	Basic Form
Walkin' and Swingin'	3/2/36	New York	60852-A	Columbia DB/MC-5023	Classics 573	*aaba*
Lotta Sax Appeal	3/2/36	New York	60854-A	Decca 1046	Classics 573	Blues/*aaba*
Git	3/3/36	New York	60861-B	Decca 931	Classics 573	16-bar Blues
Froggy Bottom	3/4/36	New York	60865-A	Columbia DB-5000	Classics 573	Blues
Bearcat Shuffle	3/4/36	New York	60866-A	Decca 1046	Classics 573	*aaba*/riff-based
Steppin' Pretty	3/4/36	New York	60867-A	Decca 931	Classics 573	*aaba*
Corky	3/7/36	New York	60876-A	Decca 772	Classics 573	*abab*
*Cloudy**	4/3/36	New York	60974-A	Decca 1208	Classics 573	Blues w/ vocal
In the Groove	2/15/37	New York	61951-A	Decca 1261	Classics 581	*aaba*
A Mellow Bit of Rhythm	7/26/37	New York	62446-A	Decca 1579	Classics 581	*aaba*
Twinklin'	2/8/38	New York	63256-A	Decca 2483	Classics 581	*aaba*
Little Joe from Chicago	2/8/38	New York	63259-A	Decca 1710	Classics 581	Blues/boogie style
Messa Stomp	9/9/38	New York	64615-A	Decca 2204	Classics 598	Blues
What's Your Story, Morning Glory?	10/25/38	New York	64699-A	Decca 3306	Classics 598	Blues w/ vocal
Dunkin' a Doughnut	12/5/38	New York	64781-A	Decca 2723	Classics 598	16-bar *aa'*
Mary's Idea	12/6/38	New York	64783-A	Decca 2326	Classics 598	*aaba*
Close to Five	3/16/39	New York	65188-A	Decca 2407	Classics 640	*aaba*
Big Jim Blues	11/15/39	New York	66880-A	Decca 2915	Classics 640	18-bar Blues
Scratchin' in the Gravel	6/25/40	New York	67894-A	Decca 3293	Classics 640	*aaba*
Big Time Crip	7/17/41	New York	69519-A	Decca 4042	Classics 681	Blues
With Benny Goodman						
Camel Hop†	11/12/37	New York	BS017042-1	Victor 25717B	Classics 899	*aaba*
Roll 'Em‡	2/15/38	Pittsburgh	11049-1A	Columbia ML4590	Columbia VCK40588	Blues

**Cloudy* from 1936 has nothing to do with *Cloudy* from 1929.

†Goodman's band played *Camel Hop* several times on radio broadcasts prior to the November 12 recording. This recording, however, is the studio version of the tune.

‡Similarly, *Roll 'Em* was played often on radio broadcasts, and several studio recordings of this tune exist, the first of which was recorded on 7 July 1937 in Hollywood (matrix PBS 09576-3; first appeared on Victor 25627B). This 15 February 1938 recording is the second such recording and has been released on Columbia CD VCK40588.

it."[63] Example 5 shows a passage from this chorus, scored for three saxophones and trumpet. Williams's tune *Roll 'Em* (1937), composed for Benny Goodman, which became a favorite arrangement in Goodman's book, was a twelve-bar blues, but accord-

63. Interview on KUON, Nebraska Educational Television, 1980 (see Dahl, *Morning Glory*, 94). Williams made a similar comment while discussing this tune in an interview from 1978: "We only had three saxophones and one trumpet and trombone, something like that. So what I did, I put a trumpet in and I had three saxophones to play four-part harmony" (see Mary Lou Williams, Interview by John S. Wilson, 49). However, in the autobiographical statement appearing in *Melody Maker* in 1954, her memory

Example 5. *Walkin' and Swingin'*, sax chorus with trumpet lead, A1/34.2–A2/9
(excerpt)

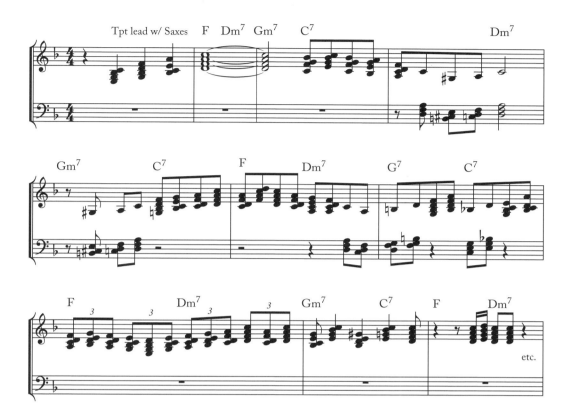

ing to Williams, it also marked the first time that boogie-woogie, always considered a piano genre, had been adapted and scored for big band. Kirk is said to have been jealous of the success Goodman's band achieved with this arrangement—after all, his chief arranger had written the tune.[64] A year later, Williams produced another boogie-woogie number for the Clouds of Joy, *Little Joe from Chicago*.

If this period of Williams's development as a composer and arranger demonstrates her assimilation of influences from other leading arrangers, it also shows her fruitful exploration of her own earlier work. Especially in the first years of this middle period, Williams found inspiration in, and drew material from, several of her own tunes from the 1929–31 era (see Table 3), providing them with fresh treatments. All five of these new arrangements exhibit Williams's knowledge of contemporary arranging techniques, even as they draw upon conventional approaches to form. None of the five projects a single formal structure. That is, while each number may be characterized as a blues, an *aaba* form, or some other familiar structure, each also deviates from its characteristic form at least once. Some of her updates served as vehicles for particular soloists in the band. *Corky* (1936), while maintaining essentially the same structure as its predecessor, *Corky Stomp* (1929; see Form Diagram 4), now featured clarinetist Johnny Harrington. *Lotta Sax Appeal* (1936) was reworked for tenor saxophonist Dick

---

of this innovative technique was mistaken: " 'Walkin' and Swingin' was one of those numbers musicians like to play. I had tried out trumpet combining with saxes to make the sound of five reeds, and this was different and effective" (see Gottlieb, *Reading Jazz*, 106). A score of *Walkin' and Swingin'* in the Mary Lou Williams Collection at the Institute of Jazz Studies, in Williams's hand, does show this passage scored for trumpet and four saxophones. It seems a reasonable hypothesis that Williams rescored the arrangement at a later date with this instrumentation in mind (though no known recording of this presumably later arrangement exists), which would explain both accounts.

64. Dahl, *Morning Glory*, 110.

Table 3. Rearrangements of older tunes

Tune	Recording Date of Original	Recording Date of Revision
Mess-a-Stomp/Messa Stomp	11/7/29	9/9/38
Lotta Sax Appeal	11/9/29	3/2/36
Corky Stomp/Corky	11/11/29	3/7/36
Froggy Bottom	11/11/29	3/4/36
Mary's Idea	4/30/30	12/6/38

Wilson (the 1929 version had been a baritone saxophone feature), and likewise follows closely the structural model of the 1929 recording, as a comparison of Form Diagram 6 with Form Diagram 3 reveals. This structure, as noted earlier, is a hybrid form combining twelve-bar blues, sixteen-bar strains, and thirty-two-bar *aaba* structures in a single number. Within each section, the instrumentation in the updated version remains faithful to that of the original arrangement: there is space for five solos, and of these, four follow the same order: saxophone, trombone, saxophone, and trumpet.[65] The first sixteen-bar strain (B1/33–48) involves the full ensemble and the tenor sax solo trading twos in a call-and-response fashion; the full ensemble plays in the *a* sections of the *aaba* structures, while the bridge (*b*) sections feature short improvised solos. Thus Williams borrows her own structure for this arrangement, but alters the outcome by providing new sustained background chords and riffs, a new shout chorus (C1/89–120), and a tag ending.

Froggy Bottom (1936), a head arrangement in its 1929 version, is a twelve-bar blues with a repeated eight-measure, riff-based strain that is inserted between blues choruses after several of them have been played (see Form Diagram 7). Williams retains more than just this structure in her updated arrangement. Both arrangements begin with a four-measure introduction. In both cases this introduction concludes with the same descending saxophone figure, and the tune proper begins with a twenty-bar (8+12) piano solo in which the first eight bars are in C minor before moving into the parallel major for the first of several blues choruses. Also retained is the order of solos: piano, saxophone (tenor substitutes for alto), trumpet, and guitar. Williams's new arrangement incorporates a chorus with lyrics she wrote herself, while replacing the chorus of collective improvisation that concluded the 1929 version with two choruses of riff-based antiphonal writing for reeds and brass.

Two years later, Williams reworked what had been another head arrangement, *Mess-a-Stomp* from 1929. The 1938 versions, now titled *Messa Stomp*, again remain faithful to the original structure, not only at the large-scale, section-by-section level, but also in the number of choruses, the solo instruments, and even the solo order (Form Diagram 8). New elements include the ensemble and sectional background riffs, which are tightly and crisply played, and the ensemble shout, expanded in the later version from one chorus to three. In the version recorded on 9 September 1938, however, Williams replaces the guitar solo with a transition that leads from the muted brass interlude into the shout chorus (see Example 6; note that the transcription from the 1938 recording given in this example contains slight differences from the parallel passage in the edited score). This passage, just four measures long, moves smartly from the preceding muted brass interlude into an octave saxophone arpeggiation that winds its

---

65. The only exception is the solo at C1, section *b*, assigned to the piano in the 1929 version, but played by the clarinet in the 1936 version.

Theodore E. Buehrer

Form Diagram 6.   *Lotta Sax Appeal* (1936)

Intro₍₄₊₄₌₈₎ A1+A2₍₁₂₊₁₂₌₂₄₎   B1+B2₍₁₆₊₁₆₌₃₂₎   A3+A4₍₁₂₊₁₂₌₂₄₎   C1₍₈₊₈₊₈₊₈₌₃₂₎   C2₍₁₆₊₈₊₈₌₃₂₎   Tag₍₃₎
         TSax solo w/   B1: ens/TSax trade 2s   Trb solo   *aa*: ens riff   *aa*: TSax solo w/
         brass bkgd   B2: TSax solo w/   *b*: Cl solo   brass bkgd
                                  brass bkgd   *a*: ens riff   (reprise of B2)
                                                                                            b: Tpt solo
                                                                                            a: ens riff

             Blues   16mm. strain, repeated Blues   *aaba*   *aaba*

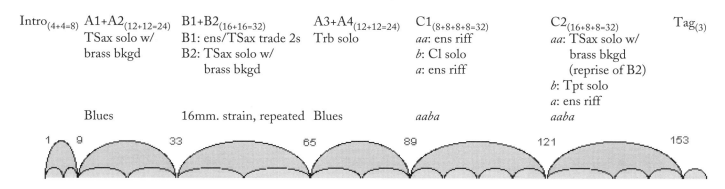

Form Diagram 7.   *Froggy Bottom* (1936)

Intro₍₄₎ A₍₈₎   B1₍₁₂₎   B2₍₁₂₎   B3₍₁₂₎   B4₍₁₂₎   B5₍₁₂₎   C₍₈₊₈₌₁₆₎   B6₍₁₂₎   B7₍₁₂₎
          Pn solo Pn solo   TSax solo   Tpt solo w/ Vocal   Gtr solo ens riff,   ens   ens call/resp
                             w/ brass   sax bkgd   chorus   repeated   call/resp   figure changes
                             bkgd   brass vs.
                                                                                     reeds

      a   Blues --- *bb*   Blues --------------------

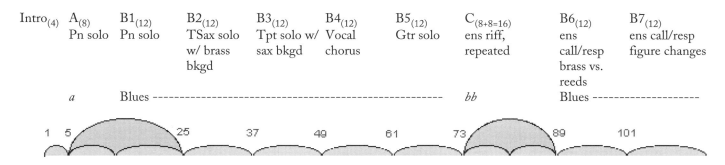

Form Diagram 8.   Comparison of three versions of *Messa Stomp*

Mess-a-Stomp (1929), recording, included as transcription in this edition

Intro₍₄₎ A1+A2₍₁₂₊₁₂₌₂₄₎   X₍₄₎   B1+B2₍₈₊₈₌₁₆₎ A3+A4₍₁₂₊₁₂₌₂₄₎   C1+C2₍₁₂₊₁₂₌₂₄₎   A5₍₁₃₎   A6₍₁₂₎   Tag₍₄₎
        Cl solo   Ban   Saxes Tpt   Pn solo   brass interlude, repeated Gtr solo   ens shout   Chord
                           fill   soli   solo
           Blues   Gm-D7 vamp------   Blues   non-Blues   Blues--------------

Messa Stomp (1938), score version 1, included in this edition

Intro₍₄₎ A1+A2₍₁₂₊₁₂₌₂₄₎   X₍₄₎   B1+B2₍₈₊₈₌₁₆₎ A3+A4₍₁₂₊₁₂₌₂₄₎   C1+C2₍₁₂₊₁₂₌₂₄₎   A5₍₁₃₎ A6₍₁₂₎ A7₍₁₂₎   A8₍₁₂₎ Tag₍₄₎
        Cl solo   Gtr   Sax   Tpt   Pn solo   muted brass interlude   Gtr   ens   shout (6) ens   Cl solo
                           fill   soli   solo   solo   shout + TSax   shout
           Blues   Gm-D7 vamp   Blues   non-Blues   Blues   solo (6)

Messa Stomp (1938), recording, not included in this edition (piano solo, however, added to score version in this edition)

        A1+A2₍₁₂₊₁₂₌₂₄₎   X1₍₄₎   B1+B2₍₈₊₈₌₁₆₎ A3+A4₍₁₂₊₁₂₌₂₄₎   C1+C2+X2₍₁₂₊₁₂₊₄₌₂₈₎   A5₍₁₂₎   A6₍₁₂₎   A7₍₁₂₎
        Cl solo   Gtr   Sax   Tpt   Pn solo   muted brass interlude   ens shout shout (6),   ens shout
                           fill   soli   solo   (12+12), transition w/   TSax
                                                                   saxes, brass not muted (4)   solo (6)
           Blues   Gm-D7 vamp   Blues   non-Blues   Blues

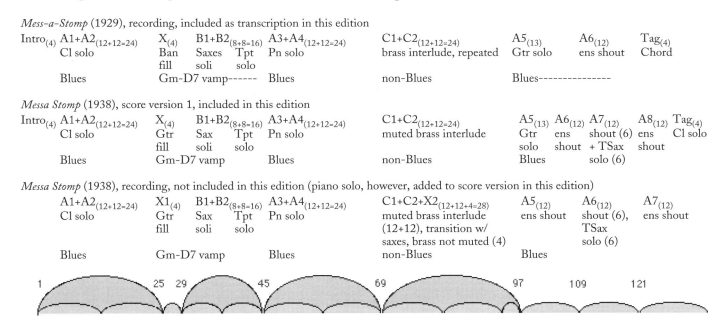

Example 6. *Messa Stomp* (1938) recording, muted brass interlude C1+C2 (mm. 69–92) and transition X2 (mm. 93–96)

way to a prolonged dominant. The brass (no longer muted) play several hits and join the extended dominant with a sustained chord of their own while the drums fill two measures in anticipation of the ensuing shout chorus. Despite its four-bar length, the passage's unexpected appearance is surprising enough to raise the tension further.

Williams's transformation of *Mary's Idea* to the 1938 versions presents the most sophisticated reworking of any tune to date. Form Diagram 9 provides the basic formal diagrams. A comparison with the original version reveals a number of similarities and some departures from it too. The tune's formal structure, thirty-two-bar *aaba*, remains intact. So does the inclusion of an interlude between the second and third choruses, as well as an emphasis on improvised solos, which are indicated in the score for

Theodore E. Buehrer

Form Diagram 9. Comparison of three versions of *Mary's Idea*

Mary's Idea (1930), recording, included as transcription in this edition

Intro(4+6=10)	A1(8+8+8=32)	A2(8+8+8=32)	X(6+8+8=22)	A3(8+8+8=32)	Tag(4)
	aa: Tpt 1 solo, tutti bkgd	aa: BSax solo/tutti trade 4s	Tutti based on *a*	*a*: Cl solo, ens w/o tpts bkgd	
	b: Saxes soli	*b*: brass soli		*a*: tutti/Cl solo trade 4s	
	a: Tpt 1 solo, tutti bkgd	*a*: tutti/BSax solo trade 4s		*b*: ASax solo, brass bkgd	
				a: tutti	

A4(8+8+8+6=30)
aa: tutti
    call/response
    w/ sax section
b: tutti
a: tutti

Mary's Idea (1938), score version, included in this edition

Intro(4)
Sax octave riff

A1(8+8+8=32)
aa: Sax octave riff/brass
    tutti lead
b: Sax soli (4), Trb solo over
    sax bkgd (4)
a: brass lead/Sax riff returns

A2(8+8+8=32)
aa: Tpt solo over tutti sax
    bkgd
b: tutti
a: Tpt solo over tutti sax bkgd

X1(8+8=16)
xx': Cl solo over
     muted brass

A3(8+8+8=32)
aa: TSax solo over muted
    brass
b: Trb solo, saxes bkgd
a: TSax solo over muted
    brass

X2(4)
y: Hemiola
   riff in
   saxes then
   add brass

A4(8+8+8=32)
aa: tutti shout with
    2nd hemiola riff
b: Trb solo (4), tutti
    riff, muted (4)
a: reprise of A1/*a*
    elided into Tag

Tag(6)

Mary's Idea (1938), recording, not part of this edition

Intro(4)
Sax octave riff

A1(8+8+8=32)
aa: Sax octave riff/brass
    tutti lead
b: Sax soli (4), Trb solo over
    sax bkgd (4)
a: brass lead/Sax riff returns

A2(8+8+8=32)
aa: Tpt solo over tutti sax
    bkgd
b: Pn solo
a: Pn solo contd

X(8+6+5=19)
x: Cl solo over
   muted brass
x': Contd
y: Hemiola riff in
   saxes then add
   brass

A3(8+8+8=32)
aa: tutti shout with
    2nd hemiola riff
b: Trb solo (4), tutti cresc.
    riff (4)
a: reprise of A1/*a*
    elided into Tag

Tag(6)

5   37   69   88   118

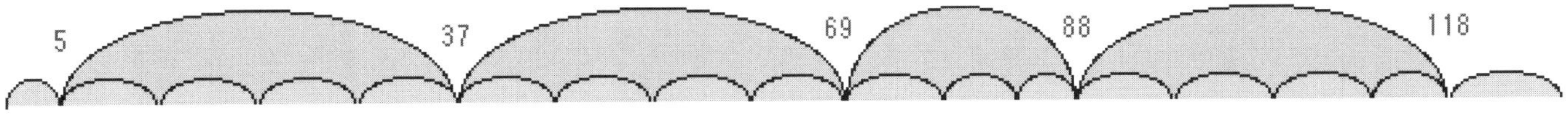

Example 7. *Mary's Idea*, comparison of head melodies (A1/1–8)

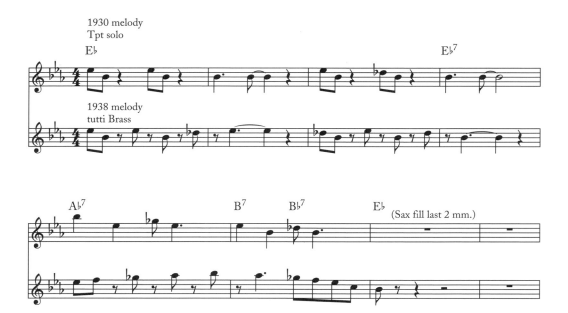

trombone, trumpet, clarinet, and tenor saxophone.[66] Example 7 reveals another parallel between the two versions: the head itself. For a tune bearing the same name as an earlier work, this comes as no surprise, but it is relevant here because the heads differ, and the transformation of one into the other is noteworthy. The 1938 version is based on the same chord progression as the original version, and the example shows that Williams drew at least the melody of the new version's *a* section from the original trumpet melody, with its repetitive bouncing between tonic and dominant in the first four bars and the ascent to bb″ in the fifth. Both versions fill the last two bars of the first *a* section with a saxophone soli, and that combination returns in the bridge of both arrangements.

Differences between the 1930 and 1938 versions of *Mary's Idea* reflect a concern for practical considerations as well as Williams's desire to experiment with conventional methods. The somewhat slower tempo of the 1938 version would have made the arrangement eminently danceable at a time when jazz music's primary function was to accompany dancers. Perhaps the slower tempo accounts for the arrangement's truncated introduction and the "missing" fourth chorus in the recording: at this tempo, only three choruses and the interlude could fit onto a three-minute recording. Other musical differences point to Williams's more highly developed grasp of the day's conventions and her ability both to write within and to stretch them. The harmonized brass melody is played against a unison saxophone riff heard first as the tune's introduction. The result is a rhythmic counterpoint between brass and reeds in which the brass play almost entirely on the offbeats, while the reed riff includes notes both on and off the beat.[67] Example 8 provides a sketch of this opening passage. Interplay between brass

---

66. In the shorter, recorded version, emphasis on improvised solos remains, but they are taken by trombone, trumpet, piano, and clarinet.

67. Martin and Waters, *Jazz: The First 100 Years*, 144. This syncopated brass riff also recalls Fletcher Henderson's brass lines in some of his early 1930s arrangements, referred to by Schuller as " 'chains' of sprightly-syncopated accents" (see Schuller, *The Swing Era*, 22). These are on display in the out chorus of Henderson's arrangement *Between the Devil and the Deep Blue Sea*, recorded in June 1935 by Benny Goodman's orchestra (available on Musidisc LP 30JA5152 and Tax CD 3708-2), and in the introduction of *Wrappin' it Up*, recorded in September 1934 by Henderson's orchestra (available on Classics 535), to mention two examples.

Theodore E. Buehrer

Example 8. *Mary's Idea* (1938), brass vs. reeds (Intro/1–4 and A1/1–7)

and reeds is stepped up considerably from the 1930 arrangement. Another difference lies in the soloists' backgrounds, which possess a life and an interest of their own. Yet another difference involves Williams's more advanced harmonic language in the later version. Though the same basic chord changes remain, chord extensions and alterations not found in the 1930 version appear in 1938.[68] Table 4 summarizes the harmonic vocabulary found in the later version. A final difference pertains to the interlude, for here Williams moves beyond convention and experiments with phrase structure, rhythm, and timbral combinations. A sketch of this interlude, as it appears in the recording, is provided in Example 9. It is here, incidentally, that Williams uses many of the extended and altered chords listed in Table 4. This passage, unlike the corresponding one in the 1930 arrangement, does not develop the *a* section but is based on new material. Williams divides the passage into three phrases of unequal length: first eight, then six, and then five measures. The first two phrases contain an improvised clarinet solo over a harmonized line played by three trumpets and a single trombone, all with cup mutes. This is the only occurrence of this timbral combination in the entire piece, and the result sounds quite refined. The second phrase, which answers the first, is truncated, as the final two bars, anticipated as a phrase ending, are elided into the passage's final phrase. The last five bars, which lead to the final chorus, present a repeating rhythmic figure that sounds as if it is in three, creating a hemiola effect against the prevailing 4/4 meter and building tension and energy that is released only when the shout chorus arrives. Incidentally, though the same material appears in the score version of this arrangement (X1), there Williams's interlude conforms to a more conventional (8+8) structure, where the second phrase is neither truncated nor elided, but moves to a cadence that launches the guitar solo.

Williams did not limit her innovative use of form to tunes she revised from earlier days. She continued to experiment, even though opportunities in Andy Kirk's band for new jazz arrangements declined in the late 1930s and early 1940s, as the band's growing popularity gave her less room for creative inspiration. Williams's arrangement of *Big Jim Blues* (1939), a feature for longtime Clouds of Joy trumpet player Harry "Big Jim" Lawson, uses an unusual eighteen-bar blues form. Even more peculiar are the subdivisions of the eighteen-measure chorus, marked by the changes of chord, as shown in Form Diagram 10. Seven measures of tonic harmony (divided into a four-measure and

---

68. This observation goes for many of the tunes Williams composed and arranged during this period, not just *Mary's Idea*.

Table 4. *Mary's Idea* (1938), summary of harmonic language

Triads	Minor 7ths	Dominant 7ths
Maj	min^7	Mm^7
min	min$^{7\flat5}$ (ø7)	Mm$^{7(+5)}$
dim		Mm$^{7\text{sus}}$
Maj^6		Mm^9
min^6		Mm$^{9(+5)}$
		Mm$^{7(\sharp9\sharp5)}$
		Mm$^{7(\sharp9\flat13)}$
		Mm^{13}
		Mm$^{7(\flat13)}$

a three-measure phrase) yield to the subdominant for three measures (the last of these bars moves to the minor subdominant). Tonic returns for four measures beginning in bar 11, and that return is followed by two measures each of dominant and tonic harmony to close the refrain. Thus, although the tune contains the essential harmonic ordering expected in a blues form, the proportions are distorted, especially within the first three chord changes (I-IV-I), creating a formal structure that, though unconventional, flows coherently.

Many of Williams's remaining compositions from this period were feature numbers, and they tend toward conventional writing. Examples include *Twinklin'* (1938) and *Close to Five* (1939), which featured the composer herself at the piano; *Cloudy* (1936), *Git* (1936), and *What's Your Story, Morning Glory?* (1938), highlighting solo vocalist Pha Terrell; and *Big Time Crip* (1941), with lyrics sung by the full ensemble (the boogie-woogie *Little Joe from Chicago*, from 1938, also includes ensemble lyrics). But even in Williams's more formally conservative efforts, her arrangements were hard-swinging (see, for example, *Walkin' and Swingin'*, *A Mellow Bit of Rhythm*, *Dunkin' a Doughnut*, or *Camel Hop*), possessing some element that made them memorable. For example, *A Mellow Bit of Rhythm* (1937) demonstrates a conventional form, achieving a dark, bluesy sound through a harmonized saxophone melody with the tenor saxophone leading (not the usual alto), drawing a contrast later with a bright clarinet obbligato duet. Through infectious melodies, rhythms, and timbres her arrangements consistently displayed a forward drive that provided energy and danceability. Benny Goodman is said to have commented, "Usually, we'd play five or six arrangements in a set and each would be three minutes. But some of those arrangements Mary Lou Williams wrote you would want to play for more than three minutes and the dancers would want you to, too."[69] Williams's composition and arranging efforts from this period placed her among the elite jazz composers of the day, at least as judged by her peers. She was held in high regard not only because of her ability to create an interesting and rhythmically effective arrangement of virtually any tune, whatever its source, but also because these arrangements successfully balanced inventive section and ensemble writing with ample room for improvised solos, together with interest-grabbing, well-crafted backgrounds that always managed to sound fresh. Her arrangements also held appeal because they consistently displayed her willingness to move

---

69. Giddins, "Mary Lou Williams," 80.

Theodore E. Buehrer

Example 9.   *Mary's Idea* (1938) recording, interlude (mm. 69–87)

Form Diagram 10.   *Big Jim Blues*

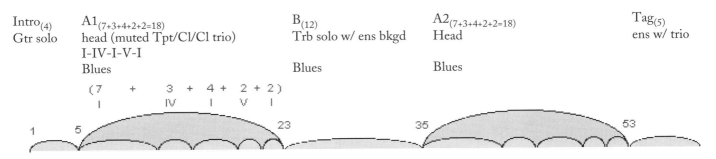

Intro(4)	A1(7+3+4+2+2=18)	B(12)	A2(7+3+4+2+2=18)	Tag(5)
Gtr solo	head (muted Tpt/Cl/Cl trio)	Trb solo w/ ens bkgd	Head	ens w/ trio
	I–IV–I–V–I			
	Blues	Blues	Blues	

beyond conventions and experiment with new forms and arranging techniques. But at the dawn of the 1940s, as opportunities for this sort of writing dwindled with the Clouds of Joy, Williams began to contemplate other musical paths.

Freelancing in New York City: 1942–52

In truth, well before her departure in 1942, Williams had grown frustrated with the limitations placed on her by Andy Kirk and the Clouds of Joy. As early as 1938–39, she was growing dissatisfied, not only with the relatively few jazz arrangements played by the band, but with other aspects of the job. The band's increasing commercial success brought a decrease in creative opportunities for Williams (and some fellow members of the band). This fact, coupled with disagreements between Williams and Kirk over band members' wages—Williams lobbied for higher wages for her bandmates, even as she was the highest paid member of the group—deepened her discontent.

> At this time I was feeling really dragged so far as Kirk's outfit went. I could not play or write my best for thinking about my share of the loot, and my sacrifices before we made a hit. All my piano solos I turned over to [guitarist] Floyd [Smith]. I had gotten sick of playing the same ones long ago. Our repertoire consisted of recorded hits, and the solos had to be exactly like those on the records.
>
> I had plenty of offers to leave, but turned them down. Though dissatisfied, I still felt loyal to the band . . . Don Byas came into the band, and now we had two great tenorman [*sic*]—Don and Dick Wilson. I think it was these two who kept me in the band, for I got real kicks out of jamming with them. I began to feel better.[70]

Williams's goodwill did not last indefinitely, however, and she left Andy Kirk and the Clouds of Joy in May of 1942, walking off the bandstand during a performance in Washington, D.C. Though she first returned to family in Pittsburgh and it appeared that her disillusioned view of jazz might keep her sidelined for some time, two weeks after her arrival trumpeter Harold "Shorty" Baker showed up in Pittsburgh unexpectedly. Baker had been in Kirk's band since 1940, and he and Williams had developed a friendship. Baker's encouragement over the ensuing weeks persuaded Williams to start performing again, and the two of them formed a combo, also including a young drummer named Art Blakey, that played regionally with some success. At the same time, the relationship between Williams and Baker had blossomed into a romance (Williams having been separated from her husband since 1938, about the time that John Williams left the Clouds of Joy). But Baker's presence in the combo was short lived, as he accepted an offer to join the Duke Ellington Orchestra on the road, and the combo struggled to find a suitable replacement. The romantic relationship continued as best it could, though Williams's and Baker's physical separation complicated matters. Unable to find a replacement for Baker in the combo, she decided to join him on the road. The two were married by December of 1942, yet this arrangement must have felt eerily familiar. Once again, Williams found herself traveling with a band as an unemployed spouse, even though by now, her musicianship proven, she had tasted stardom with Kirk's band. She persisted for six months, providing arrangements for Ellington's band during this time, but by the middle of 1943 her frustration mounted again, exacerbated by marital conflict (physical abuse is said to have been involved), and she made a clean break from a tumultuous, short-lived marriage and from the road, moving to New York to restart her own career. Though both Williams and Baker made attempts to reconcile, they were never able to rekindle their relationship, so their separation became permanent. Williams spent the rest of the 1940s as a freelance musician, fronting trios,

---

70. Mary Lou Williams, "Autobiography," 109. It is unclear whether jamming with Don Byas and Dick Wilson was included in the working life of Andy Kirk and his Clouds of Joy or took place during off-the-job moments.

leading combos, performing as a soloist, and, much less frequently, composing and arranging for big bands.

No longer in the employ of a working, touring band, and therefore no longer needing to supply fresh big band arrangements on a regular basis, Williams's compositions and arrangements for big band diminished during this period. It is worth noting that her departure from the Clouds of Joy in 1942 corresponds to the United States' involvement in World War II, a recording ban imposed by American Federation of Musicians president James Petrillo in August of that year (lasting until late 1944), and a time of changing artistic tastes and aesthetic goals, particularly among African American jazz musicians.[71] These developments led to the decline of the Swing Era and a significant decrease in the number of big bands. The concomitant decrease in Williams's writing for big band reflects changing economic realities. The best known of the big bands, including those led by Duke Ellington and Benny Goodman, survived, and Williams supplied both of them (and others) with music during the 1940s. But whereas this kind of composition and arranging had supplied the bulk of her income in the 1930s and the early 40s, freelancing in the remainder of the 1940s required a wider variety of musical activities. Ultimately, the continued decline in the popularity of big band music and other factors affected Williams's compositional future, and after 1949 she wrote very little music for this medium.

While the New York jazz scene was dominated by male musicians (as was the case everywhere she went), Williams quickly found a niche among the musical progressives there. Like many others, she was attracted to bebop, which by the mid- to late 1940s had emerged from the crucible of after-hours clubs like Minton's Playhouse, finding a toehold as the newest jazz style. Upon her arrival in New York, she became a regular at Minton's, though by her own admission she played less often than others. By the fall of 1943 she was offered a regular engagement leading a piano trio at the progressive, racially integrated Café Society club, owned by Barney Josephson, which frequently gave female entertainers top billing, including jazz musicians like Billie Holiday, Lena Horne, Hazel Scott, and Sarah Vaughan. These connections helped her to befriend many of the musicians now considered originators of the new style, including Thelonious Monk and Dizzy Gillespie, and her apartment at Hamilton Terrace in Harlem (near Minton's) became the place to go after the clubs closed. As Williams describes,

> After finishing work at Café [Society] each morning, I'd either pick up several musicians and take them along with me or else we would meet at my apartment when I got home around 4 o'clock. The guys used to come to my house then—Bud Powell, Tadd Dameron, Monk, Miles, Mel Tormé, Sarah Vaughan, Dizzy—all the boppers. Even Benny Goodman . . . [We] would write music and play all morning, almost 'til it was time to go to work. Sometimes Tadd Dameron would get stuck with his arrangements and he'd say, "Come on and play something, Lou." And while I was creating, it would push him off again. And Aaron Bridgers and Billy Strayhorn, plus various disc jockeys and newspapermen, would be in and out of my place at all hours, and we'd really ball.[72]

Williams also recalled the mentoring she would do with the younger bebop musicians such as Monk, Dameron, and Powell: "[Most] of them needed inspiration and they wrote the music up here at the house . . . Tadd Dameron and all the cats used to come. Monk used to come here and write his music. I have some music he left here

---

71. For more information about the 1942–44 recording ban, see the entry for "Petrillo, James Caesar" in *Encyclopedia of Popular Music*. The seeds of bebop were being sown at this time as well. Among the many studies of the development of this music, DeVeaux's *The Birth of Bebop* is strongly recommended. See Chapter 4, "Spitballs and Tricky Riffs."

72. Dahl, *Morning Glory*, 185. An edited version of this diary entry appears in Mary Lou Williams, "Autobiography," 113.

now—and Bud [Powell]. If they wrote at home they'd bring it here for me to hear it and see how I liked it."[73]

Williams's music—both her compositions and her arrangements—began to adopt some of the traits of the bebop language: disjunct melodic lines; chromatically extended and altered harmonies; and varied, unexpected background hits and rhythmic figures. These influences can be detected as early as 1944 in a tune such as *Gjon Mili Jam Session*, which she was able to record with a seven-piece combo due to a fortuitous relationship she forged with independent studio owner and producer Moses ("Moe") Asch, who gave his clients *carte blanche* in the way of creative license:

> It was different because Moe Asch had more love and he had more respect for jazz artists. Often he would take us to dinner, the nicest dinners, steak dinners, the nicest places and it was his idea that an artist should be heard if they're talented. He'd turn the tape on and go away, let you record anything you wanted to record, and it always worked out great.[74]

Although the list of Williams's original compositions for big band during this time is relatively short (shown in Table 5), it tells only part of the story. Her compositional efforts expanded to include not only works for this genre, but also for the combos she led, as well as an ambitious larger work for symphony orchestra and jazz combo, the *Zodiac Suite* from 1945.[75] Williams's work with big bands during this period focused mostly on Duke Ellington's and Benny Goodman's orchestras, for which she provided many arrangements (including a masterful, hard-driving swing arrangement of Irving Berlin's *Blue Skies* from 1943 for Ellington's orchestra) and fewer original compositions.[76] The bebop influence in her big band writing becomes apparent in Williams's compositions later in the decade, however. In *Whistle Blues*, a tune that in fact is an *aaba* structure, Williams begins innocuously enough, with a simple head that is actually whistled by the band in unison while the rhythm section plays an easy, two-beat accompaniment. But the bridge melody of the arrangement she wrote for the Milton Orent-Frank Roth Orchestra, played by the full ensemble, is a harbinger of the new influence, full of chromatically altered voicings and angular melodic lines (see excerpt in Example 10).[77] By the middle of this number, with a trumpet soloing over whole-tone harmonic background figures supplied by the ensemble, further proof of bebop's influence may be heard.

The culmination of Williams's involvement with the bebop style in her big band writing can be heard in her composition *In the Land of Oo-Bla-Dee* (lyrics by Milton Orent),[78] which in 1949 she arranged for Dizzy Gillespie and his bebop-styled big

---

73. Mary Lou Williams, Interview by John S. Wilson, 103. Further musical evidence of Williams's influence on Monk is that a passage in the middle of her big band arrangement of *Walkin' and Swingin'* from 1936 later became the first four measures of Monk's tune *Rhythm-a-Ning*, which he recorded in 1957.

74. Mary Lou Williams, Interview by John S. Wilson, 77. *Gjon Mili Jam Session* was first recorded on 5 June 1944 on Asch (552-2; matrix 1236), and has been reissued on Classics 814 (CD). Williams had six recording sessions with Asch in 1944 (listed in the release of *Mary Lou Williams, 1944*, Classics 814), which took place during the recording ban. Asch, like many small, independent recording labels, sprang up during the ban (which affected the larger recording companies), providing musicians with opportunities to record.

75. The 31 December 1945 concert performance of *Zodiac Suite* was recorded and has been reissued on compact disc as Jazz Classics Records JZCL-6002.

76. Williams's arrangement of *Blue Skies* can be heard on Circle CCD-101. Shortly after leaving the Clouds of Joy in 1942, Williams joined Ellington's band on the road, staying for approximately six months. During this time she wrote several arrangements, playing with the band only occasionally. See Kernodle, *Soul on Soul*, 89–90.

77. The arrangement for Goodman, recorded in the same year (1947), is substantially different, lacking the bridge and final *a* section altogether on the head chorus (though Goodman solos over the *aaba* form). The arrangement is less adventuresome harmonically than the one for Orent.

78. On the first page of a sheet music publication, Criterion Music Co., 1949 (red cover, Capitol Songs Inc.), words and music of *In the Land of Oo-Bla-Dee* are credited jointly to Williams and Milton Orent. However, private correspondence with Peter O'Brien, S.J., executive director of the Mary Lou Williams Foundation, indicates that Orent provided only the lyrics that accompany this tune.

Theodore E. Buehrer

Table 5.   Williams's original compositions for big band, 1943–49

Title	Band	Recording Date	Original Recording	CD Reissue
Shorty Boo Blues	DE	c. 1943	N/A	N/A
Whistle Blues	BG	1/28/47	Capitol 374	Capitol 32086
	MO	c. 1947	Asch Disc 6067B	Classics 1050
Lonely Moments	DE	c. 1943	N/A	N/A
	BG	1/28/47	Capitol 374	Capitol 32086
	MO	c. 1947	Asch Disc 6067A	Classics 1050
	DE	c. 1947	N/A	N/A
In the Land of Oo-Bla-Dee	DG	7/6/49	Victor	Victor 09026-68517-2

Key. BG = Benny Goodman Orchestra; DE = Duke Ellington Orchestra; DG = Dizzy Gillespie Orchestra; MO = Milton Orent Orchestra

Example 10.   *Whistle Blues* (arrangement for Orent, 1947); mm. 25–28 (bridge excerpt)

band, who recorded it in July of that year. (A transcription of this recording is included in this edition.) Williams kept busy with this tune throughout 1949, first recording it in March with a combo of her own—vocalist, trumpet, flute, bass clarinet, guitar, piano, bass, drums—that show her exploring timbres that included traditional orchestral instruments. She followed that version with a fresh arrangement for Benny Goodman's combo, who recorded it in April. Her arrangement for Gillespie was also new, and full of bop idioms. The head displays a wealth of disjunct motion (note the frequent tritone leaps) and angular contours, and the arrangement complements the melodic line, with its frequent dissonant brass punches and jagged countermelodies (Example 11).[79]

If *In the Land of Oo-Bla-Dee* represents Williams's embrace of the melodic and harmonic language of bebop, her composition *Lonely Moments* shows her fusing this style with other musical influences that were swirling around her. The composition was conceived in 1943 and bears a copyright date from that year, and its first arrangement appears to have been intended for the Duke Ellington Orchestra, though they

79. My own transcription uncovers significant differences in the chords and voicings throughout this passage in comparison to Lopeman's transcription. A score in Williams's hand also exists, but it bears the words "based off Dizzy Gillespie's Victor recording" across the top of the first page, indicating that, rather than the original score, Williams wrote it down after the fact. A quick comparison of it to the recording reveals many differences that bear out this hypothesis.

Example 11. *In the Land of Oo-Bla-Dee*, head with backgrounds (simplified reduction of A1/1–14)

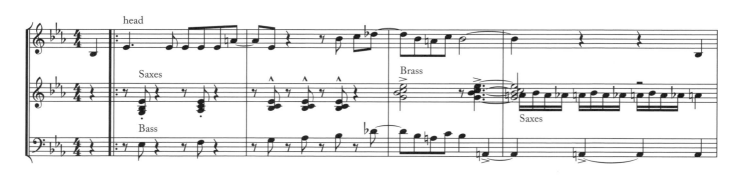

never recorded it. No performances of this tune have been documented before December 1945, when Williams gave a live performance of a new combo arrangement, following it in February 1946 with a solo piano presentation. These early versions offered a thirty-two-bar *aaba* structure containing a bridge that was either written out (in the arrangement for Ellington, and the combo arrangement) or improvised (in the solo piano version). Williams revamped the tune for Benny Goodman's big band later that year, and it was premiered in November. Goodman had begun to experiment with his band's book at this time, feeling that his music had grown stale and was in need of a change. Though he had scoffed "Oh, bebop!" when Williams first delivered her arrangement, demanding that she change some of the more harmonically complex passages, it still retained much of its modern flavor.[80] She had composed a new bridge: another typical bop melody line played in octaves by brass over sustained saxophone background chords, as well as backgrounds for Goodman's solo. These backgrounds

---

80. Firestone, *Swing, Swing, Swing*, 339. Goodman's distaste for bebop's angularity and dissonant harmonies was well known. For further context for this quote, see Firestone, 328–32.

Theodore E. Buehrer

vary, some being chordal and others linear, but all show similar leanings toward the bebop idiom: the chords include dissonant clusters and chromatic extensions. Often articulated on offbeats, the melodic backgrounds tend toward short unison punches that, like the bridge melody, are angular and disjunct. An unrecorded version of this work, similar in style to the arrangement for Goodman, was completed in 1947 for Ellington's orchestra and is included in this volume, edited from a surviving manuscript.

Williams's avid listening, dating from her formative years in Kansas City, had continued into the 1940s, and she was drawn increasingly not only to bebop but also to classical music, including both modernists and the historical Western musical canon. During these years she formed a close relationship with bassist and NBC studio arranger Milton Orent, who had organized the orchestra Williams recorded with in 1947, and whom she had first met in the late 1930s when he did some work for the Clouds of Joy. About Orent, Williams said,

> I studied with Milt. In the latter part of 1945 we used to visit the library on East 58th Street and listen to music with earphones, reading scores—Hindemith, Schoenberg, Berg and all of the German composers. Milt made a present of a few scores and records. The reason I was so ahead in modern harmony was that I absorbed from him. He knew so much about chords and things. He knew a great deal about Schoenberg, Hindemith, and others before it became the thing. After being around him awhile I decided to dig intellectual music.[81]

Later, Williams declared Orent "about 30 years ahead in sound," adding that "he was so far out they [NBC] finally fired him."[82] Bearing in mind Williams's commitment to musical exploration and innovation throughout her career, in 1946 her growing interest in sound and color surfaced in a big band arrangement of the movement titled *Scorpio* from *Zodiac Suite*, which appears in this edition. Written with Ellington's band in mind, this arrangement is filled with densely packed, sometimes dissonant harmonies, experimenting with a variety of harmonic colors throughout. Although he may have had his band read the arrangement, he never recorded it. *Lonely Moments* may be seen as another canvas on which Williams tried out her growing knowledge of classical techniques. Williams was far from alone in her search for new sounds. By the late 1940s and the 1950s more and more jazz composers and performers were looking for ways to frame their music as art, and drawing on musical techniques from the European tradition was a way for her to move in that direction. She had already begun to merge bebop with classical elements, as her *Zodiac Suite* and her timbral explorations in the combo arrangement of *In the Land of Oo-Bla-Dee* illustrate. But in both the Goodman and the Ellington versions of *Lonely Moments* she follows the improvised solo passage with a fugal exposition for the ensemble that leads to the climax of the piece: an eight-bar shout passage based on new material (Example 12) and then repeated.[83] Based on a bop-oriented fugue subject, the exposition follows standard common-practice technique, structurally and harmonically. A four-measure subject entry, played by unison trumpets, is followed by a two-measure bridge that modulates to the minor dominant for the second subject entry, played by saxophones in octaves. The trumpets continue with a countersubject against the saxes, while the bridge returns to the tonic key for the third subject entry, played by unison trombones. The saxophones faithfully reproduce the countersubject against the trombones, while the trumpets play in free counterpoint against the two lower parts. The exposition breaks off only to prepare for the subsequent climax (m. 103). This passage recalls Bill

---

81. Dahl, *Morning Glory,* 163–64.
82. Morgenstern, liner notes.
83. The fugue passage presented here is the same which can be found in section C of the arrangement for Duke Ellington, presented in this edition.

Example 12. *Lonely Moments*, fugue exposition (arrangement for Benny Goodman, 1947), mm. 85 (with upbeat)–102 and beginning of next passage in m. 103

Finegan's arrangement of *Song of the Volga Boatmen* for Glenn Miller, with its canonic brass and reed duet toward the end that builds to a peak of intensity. Although there is no evidence of it, it is not unreasonable to imagine that Williams, ardent student of such music as she was, drew some measure of inspiration from this arrangement as well.[84] Quite simply, although Williams did not mention Bach or other Baroque-era

84. *Song of the Volga Boatmen* was first recorded by the Glenn Miller Orchestra in December of 1940 as a part of NBC's "Café Rouge" Hotel Pennsylvania broadcast (available on Reader's Digest CD 3979). Miller's first studio recording of this arrangement, made in January 1941 (matrix 058885-1), was first

Theodore E. Buehrer

composers by name, it is clear that her studies included that period of Western music history, and that she worked diligently to incorporate what she learned into a jazz idiom.

Much as she would do two years later with *In the Land of Oo-Bla-Dee*, Williams spent considerable time working on new versions of *Lonely Moments* in 1947. She wrote two more arrangements in the ensuing months: in addition to the Goodman and Ellington versions (the first recorded by Goodman in January 1947, and Ellington's version shortly thereafter which was not recorded), she produced a version for Orent's studio orchestra as well as a combo arrangement for Benny Goodman, scored for two clarinets, tenor saxophone, and rhythm section. Goodman never recorded this combo version of the tune. Indeed, it seems to have been left unfinished.[85] Orent's tentette, however, did record *Lonely Moments* in 1947.[86] A full discussion of these versions, published in another article, is not repeated here, except to say that Williams must have been fascinated by contrapuntal technique at this time, because she wrote entirely different fugue subjects and expositions for both the Orent and the Goodman combo arrangements.[87] The remaining two appear as Examples 13a and 13b.[88]

In some ways the decade of the 1940s stands as a pinnacle of Williams's professional career. She enjoyed wide name recognition, and with the help of a manager was able to remain in demand as a performer in and around New York and sustain a successful career as a musician. She was also a sought-after, highly respected arranger and composer for prominent big bands. Moreover, in both arenas she was free to explore the kind of music she wanted to pursue. Her working relationship with Moses Asch gave her the luxury of recording her music as she chose, and her informal score study with Milton Orent (whose relationship with Williams eventually blossomed into a romantic one, if only briefly) led her composing in new directions.[89]

Changing Circumstances: From Europe to the University, 1952–81

Toward the end of this productive decade, however, Williams's fortunes changed, and after 1949, she stopped writing for big band for a number of years. While the biographical narrative of this period in Williams's life is fascinating, it diverges from the subject of this edition and is covered by her biographers. Therefore, I have taken a more general approach in the paragraphs that follow, providing just enough context to

---

issued as Bluebird 11029 and has been reissued on many CDs. See, for example, Bluebird/RCA 82876692412.

85. Parts for this arrangement (in Williams's hand) are housed in the Benny Goodman Papers at Yale University. The tune was arranged for two clarinets, tenor saxophone, and rhythm section (piano, guitar, bass, and drums). Goodman's part is missing, but what remains, particularly the fugue passage, appears to be a rough draft. The fugal passage is very dissonant, even by Williams's experimental standards at the time, making it hard to imagine that Goodman's combo would have ever played the arrangement, let alone recorded it.

86. The Orent-Roth studio orchestra was called a "tentette" because of its size—four saxes (alto, two tenors, and baritone), three trumpets, and a rhythm section of three (piano, bass, drums)—rather than its instrumentation.

87. See Buehrer, "*Lonely Moments?* The Anatomy of Mary Lou Williams' Oft-Recorded Tune."

88. A wealth of scores, score fragments, sets of parts, and transcriptions exist in the Mary Lou Williams Collection for *Lonely Moments*. The fugal passage from the arrangement for Benny Goodman (Example 12) is my transcription, as neither a score nor a transcription exists for this arrangement. Because the original score of the arrangement for the Orent/Roth orchestra is lacking, it too is also my transcription (Example 13a), corresponding to the transcription by Mark Lopeman. Finally, the fugal passage from the arrangement for Goodman's combo (Example 13b) is taken from parts in Williams's hand that exist in the Benny Goodman Papers at Yale University.

89. Williams's relationship with Orent is mentioned in both biographies about her. See Dahl, *Morning Glory*, 163–65, and Kernodle, *Soul on Soul*, 126–28. Peter O'Brien also has expressed his opinion in personal correspondence that Williams's relationship with Orent was—at least briefly—a romantic one.

Example 13a.   *Lonely Moments*, fugue exposition for Milton Orent-Frank Roth Orchestra, 1947 (mm. 71–82)

continue the narrative while reducing the level of detail and documentation.[90] Williams continued to book club engagements, while pressing her management to find better bookings with fees commensurate with her experience and talent. Debts began to mount. She spent time and energy corresponding with recording companies, trying to collect unpaid royalties. In the fall of 1952, when an opportunity for a nine-day trip to England arose, she accepted the invitation, believing that this trip, which promised to make her the headline act at an event in London that would also break a thirty-year ban on American and English jazz musicians playing together, could reinvigorate her career.[91] But the trip was built on false pretenses, concocted by agents who wished to exploit Williams's fame for their monetary gain.[92] Her financial woes continued, even as she stayed active in London, sometimes billed as the Grand Dame of Jazz, and she earned the respect of many fans. She eventually moved to the Left Bank in Paris to take advantage of the active jazz scene there.[93] This move also brought

90. Readers interested in more detailed accounts of this period may consult Kernodle (from Chapter 8) and Dahl (from Chapter 14), as well as Williams's own recollections in the Interview by John S. Wilson.

91. Mary Lou Williams, Interview by John S. Wilson, 79. See also Kernodle, *Soul on Soul*, 151, and Dahl, *Morning Glory*, 221–22.

92. Kernodle, *Soul on Soul*, 153. The event's planner, Harry Dawson, had proven to be unscrupulous. He changed the terms of arrangements already agreed to, booking Cab Calloway as the headline act and planning for Williams to receive second or third billing.

93. Kernodle, *Soul on Soul*, 165–67. While the development of jazz in Paris between the two world wars is well researched, relatively little has been written about the Parisian jazz scene in the post-WWII era. Two exceptions are Vihlen's "Sounding French: Jazz in Postwar France" (2000) and "Jammin' on the Champs-Elysées: Jazz, France, and the 1950s" (2000).

Theodore E. Buehrer

Example 13b. *Lonely Moments*, fugue exposition, arrangement for Goodman (combo), 1947

her closer to musicians like tenor saxophonist Don Byas and fellow pianist Garland Wilson. She had known Byas, of course, for years, dating back to her days with the Clouds of Joy, but she only met Wilson in 1952 upon her arrival in London. Wilson had spent considerable time living and performing in Europe in the 1930s, returned to the United States at the end of the decade, and again performed extensively in London and Paris after 1951.[94] Wilson and Williams formed a close relationship (though not a romantic one, for Wilson was gay), often sharing billings at clubs and sharing hotel accommodations as well. Despite regular bookings in Paris, this move failed to provide Williams with the professional satisfaction and financial stability she sought. She earnestly desired to return to the States, but could not afford a ticket home. Williams's frustration and depression culminated in the summer of 1954 when Wilson fell into poor health and died suddenly. Revealing her loneliness and personal insecurities,

94. Rye, "Wilson, Garland (Lorenzo)."

Wilson's death caused Williams to withdraw from an engagement at Paris's Le Boeuf sur le Toit nightclub, where she had succeeded him. Soon, however, she felt unwanted.

> [H]e [Wilson] was working in the Boeuf sur le Toit and certain people they didn't allow to work in there, especially a woman. Not didn't allow but they just didn't go for women as much as they did men. So what I did was to take over his job and they loved me because they loved Garland, not because I was Mary but because they loved him.[95]

She retreated to the country home of her Parisian drummer, Gérard Pochonet. (As she had done twelve years previously in Washington, D.C., ending her long connection with the Clouds of Joy, she walked off the bandstand during a performance in the Parisian nightclub.) By the end of that year, friends arranged for her passage back to New York, and what was to have been a nine-day excursion to London came to an end.

Williams had sunk into a depressed state during the days she spent in the French countryside, but she also experienced a spiritual awakening that would bring her comfort and strength. She began reading the Psalms and praying for hours on end. Upon her return to New York in December 1954, she began to attend a Catholic church and was eventually baptized in May 1957. In the meantime, she had ceased nearly all her musical endeavors, feeling called to assist fellow jazz musicians who were addicted to drugs and alcohol. "Something carried me away," she later recalled in an interview. "I began praying and I never thought about playing any more. I just thought about helping people other than—as I understand and have experienced that God was helping many souls through music, but I decided to help them in [the] flesh instead of playing for them."[96] Just as she had done for musicians in the 1940s, she opened her apartment to those who wanted or needed assistance, except that now her assistance was material rather than musical. With some money coming in from royalties and some help from friends, including Dizzy Gillespie and his wife, Lorraine, Williams's apartment served as a makeshift "halfway house" for musicians in need.[97] She provided them with food, clothing, and shelter, and assisted them in securing gigs. Eventually, as her financial situation became dire, and with the prodding of Gillespie and Fathers John Crowley and Anthony Woods, who persuaded her that she could help people the most by using the talents God had given her, Williams resumed her performance career with an appearance at the 1957 Newport Jazz Festival.[98] As she secured more engagements, she expanded her vision for this calling, establishing in 1958 the Bel Canto Foundation, a nonprofit organization through which she sought to maintain a staffed addiction recovery center with music facilities to allow the patients to continue playing during their stays.[99] The center never materialized, however. In a constant search for ways to raise additional funding for the foundation, Williams also opened in 1958 the first of a series of thrift shops, where she sold donated clothing and other goods. By the early 1960s, she had begun focusing her compositional energies on sacred music written in a jazz idiom. The result was a body of music for the church that included not only sacred songs and anthems, but also three settings of the Catholic Mass.[100]

---

95. Mary Lou Williams, Interview by John S. Wilson, 141.

96. Ibid., 149.

97. Ibid., 147.

98. Kernodle, *Soul on Soul*, 188. The performance was recorded by Norman Granz, and remains available today on compact disc as *Dizzy Gillespie at Newport* (Verve/Polygram 7476274).

99. Ibid., 191–92.

100. Williams's first attempt to compose sacred jazz yielded *A Hymn in Honor of St. Martin De Porres* in 1963 (later renamed *Black Christ of the Andes*), an anthem for a cappella voices with a brief piano interlude. Another anthem, *The Devil*, followed that same year, as did *Animi Christi*, through collaboration with jazz trombonist and composer-arranger Melba Liston. Encouraged by the priests she had befriended, Williams composed her first setting of the Mass (titled simply *Mass*) in 1967. This multi-movement composition set English translations of the Mass Ordinary (Kyrie, Gloria, Credo, Sanctus, and Agnus Dei)

Theodore E. Buehrer

Williams's resurrected performance career in the late 1950s and 1960s was intended as a means to support herself and her spiritual endeavors. Financial struggles persisted, but they did not deter Williams from pursuing this new calling to serve those in need. She hustled to make ends meet, but an extended engagement at the Hickory House club in New York, beginning in 1964, helped to keep her afloat. This nightly gig also gave her the opportunity to meet a man who would become an important figure in her life: Peter O'Brien. At the time a young seminarian on his way to becoming a Jesuit priest, O'Brien had read about Williams in a 1964 *Time* magazine article, and he decided to visit the Hickory House to listen. He befriended Williams and over time she began to depend on him. By 1970, she invited him formally to be her manager, though in fact he had been serving in that capacity unofficially since 1967. O'Brien became a stabilizing force in Williams's life and career, helping her to secure performing engagements, promoting her sacred jazz, and advocating for her causes.

Absent from Williams's musical activity during this time, however, was any writing or arranging for big bands. Williams's shift points to a changing musical marketplace. She discovered that she could pay her bills and manage her foundation more effectively through nightclub and concert engagements than by writing arrangements for a diminishing big band scene.[101] Because her focus during this time remained religious and humanitarian, serving fellow musicians in need, her return to the performance scene had more to do with raising financial support for these efforts than with personal ambitions to re-engage with jazz audiences. Thus an economic opportunity drew her back to the big band genre in 1967, when a chance to supply Count Basie and Woody Herman with a few arrangements emerged. She also pursued her old friend Duke Ellington, meeting with him during his August engagement at the Rainbow Room and following up their conversation with a pointed letter. Williams had some new material for him, she reported, but that was not all. She also asked that his publishing company return the rights of a work she had written for him unless her authorship of it was going to be compensated. And she requested an advance on the music she would be sending him:

> 8/21/67
> Dearest Duke:
> Received a call from Inez Cavanaugh last night. Seems that many of your ardent fans would like me to write for your band. I have already started a few things and hope to get them to you before you leave New York.
> Was reluctant, due to the fact I am trying madly to do something about my compositions that I have in Cecilia Publishing company [Williams's company]. I asked [Tempo Music, Ellington's publishing company] for the return of "You Know Baby" because I

---

and included additional movements that functioned as prelude ("O.W."), prayer ("Our Father"), and postlude ("Act of Contrition"). Her *Mass for Lenten Season* was the result of a commission and was completed in 1968. This work, also in English, borrowed and adapted music from the first mass setting, while following traditional Lenten Mass practice of excluding a setting of the Gloria text, and including a number of movements that fall outside of the Mass Ordinary. A third setting, *Mass for Peace* (also referred to as *Music for Peace*), was written in 1969. *Mass for Peace* included English settings of the Mass Ordinary but also expanded upon this framework with the inclusion of many additional movements. Again, some music included in *Mass for Peace* was borrowed or adapted from the earlier masses. Though Williams pursued an audience with Pope Paul VI, even traveling to the Vatican in 1968, no such meeting ever materialized. Nevertheless, her masses had strong support from leaders in the Catholic Church in the United States and were well received by congregations in their premieres. For more detailed accounts and descriptions of Williams's sacred jazz music, see Pickeral, "The Masses of Mary Lou Williams"; Kernodle, "Anything You Are Shows Up in Your Music: Mary Lou Williams and the Sanctification of Jazz"; and Kernodle's biography of Williams, *Soul on Soul* (especially Chapter 11).

101. The decline of the big band is chronicled in histories of jazz. Examples include Schuller, *The Swing Era*; Gioia, *The History of Jazz*; DeVeaux and Giddins, *Jazz*; and Martin and Waters, *Jazz: The First 100 Years*.

have spent a great deal of loot trying to do something about it and at last it was used in a Frankie Sinatra film a few months ago. I called Ruth [Duke Ellington's sister] several times to help with the exploitation. You do realize that this is unfair for the artist to do all the work . . .

. . . Well to make a long story short, I have earned very little in the past year and to be able to arrange for a band without a goodsized [*sic*] advance of money would put me in really bad shape.

I love writing for you because you are my favorite but, I will have to receive some kind of compensation. I have bills to pay. If I had money I'd write for you and not charge you anything . . .[102]

Soon thereafter, Williams mailed several arrangements of original compositions to Ellington. Table 6 gives a complete list of arrangements she wrote during this period. Although it is not known which ones were included in her mailing to Ellington, manuscripts for all on the list except *Aries Mood* and *Chunka Lunka* exist in the Duke Ellington Archives in Washington, D.C. Williams was never paid for any of these arrangements, and, judging from the clean, like-new appearance of the parts that exist in the archive, Ellington's band performed them only infrequently, if at all.[103] The list reveals Williams's continuing involvement with the twelve-bar blues. Four of the seven compositions use or modify this form, and the other three, though possessing *aaba* forms, rely heavily on the blues scale and on blues licks in their melodies. Williams had long believed that the roots of jazz lay in blues music and spirituals. Indeed, later in life she often lamented that contemporary popular music had moved away from those roots, making it necessary (in her mind) to educate audiences about the history of the music.[104] Indeed, Williams sometimes found her own life taking on the character of a blues saga. At the moment, despite her dedication to serving those in need through her thrift shop, both the shop and the Bel Canto Foundation were losing money and would close by 1968.[105] She fought an uphill battle trying to gain an audience for her jazz mass with the Vatican, and she had lost two close confidants from her local church, Father Anthony Woods (who passed away in 1965) and Brother Mario Hancock (who was transferred by his order to Rome shortly thereafter). In addition, she carried a burden of worry about her mother's deteriorating health back in Pittsburgh (she was dying of cancer) and her sister's attempted suicide.[106]

When an opportunity to open a new jazz club in Copenhagen, Denmark, was offered to Williams in 1968, she accepted, taking a number of new big band compositions with her, including *Gravel (Truth)*, *O.W.*, *New Musical Express*, *You Know, Baby*, and *Chunka Lunka*.[107] Each of these was performed on a radio broadcast by the Danish Radio Jazz Orchestra, with Williams and tenor saxophonist Ben Webster, among others, sitting in as guest performers.[108] Although she had long been away from

---

102. Excerpt from carbon copy of letter in Williams's hand, Mary Lou Williams Collection.

103. Dahl, *Morning Glory*, 297.

104. For example, in an interview conducted in 1980 by D. Antoinette Handy, Williams said, "Jazz was created out of suffering by the early black American slaves . . . it is important to have the spiritual and blues feeling in the music" ("Conversation with Mary Lou Williams," 201). Later in the interview, Williams lamented that "it seems that these young people don't know anything about jazz" (207). In response to Handy's observation that Williams displayed disdain for "commercial rock" among other things, Williams replied, "Right! . . . Those things have almost destroyed jazz" (208).

105. Kernodle, *Soul on Soul*, 221.

106. Ibid., 224.

107. The arrangements dating from this period were not recorded in Williams's lifetime. However, two recent recordings of selected compositions for big band by Williams include music from this period: Challenge CR73251 (*Rediscovered Music of Mary Lou Williams: The Lady Who Swings the Band*, 2005) and Altissimo 62102 (*The Legacy of Mary Lou Williams*, 2011).

108. The radio broadcast was not issued as a commercial recording, though a recorded copy of the broadcast resides in the Mary Lou Williams Collection at the Institute of Jazz Studies. Williams and

Theodore E. Buehrer

Table 6. Williams's compositions arranged for big band, c. 1967–68

Tune	Basic Form
Aries Mood	through-composed ("avant-garde blues")
Chunka Lunka	12-bar Blues
Chief (a.k.a. *Chief Natoma from Tacoma*)	12-bar Blues
New Musical Express (N.M.E.)	12-bar Blues
O.W.	*aaba* (solos on 12-bar Blues)
Gravel (Truth) (reworking of *Scratchin' in the Gravel*)	*aaba* (ballad)
You Know, Baby	*aaba* (ballad)

big band composing, the arrangements demonstrate her most sophisticated writing to date. *Gravel (Truth)* is a completely revised and renamed arrangement of *Scratchin' in the Gravel*, a swing composition she had written nearly three decades earlier for the Clouds of Joy (recorded in 1940).[109] Intended as a feature number for Ellington's long-time alto saxophonist, Johnny Hodges, it is repackaged as a lush ballad, rich with colorful reharmonizations and a brief, fast-waltz middle section. As just one of many examples of Williams's advanced harmonic vocabulary, Example 14 compares the opening phrase of the bridge (since no score of the 1940 version exists, this figure includes my transcription from the recording) with the corresponding passage from the 1967 version. Not only does Williams replace a tenor saxophone improvisation with a written saxophone soli, but she updates the tune's harmonic vocabulary.

Aries Mood, represented in this edition, with its abrupt tempo changes and strong ostinato bass line, is another example of her mature writing from this period.[110] The arrangement presents an abstraction of the blues form of which Williams was so fond. Subtitled "A Portrait of Ben Webster," the piece was written specifically for the Danish Radio Jazz Orchestra broadcast on which Webster performed. Williams's description scribbled on the score reads "Bop Avante [*sic*] Blues," and as such is completely unrelated to the movement titled *Aries* from her *Zodiac Suite*. As shown in Example 15, it is difficult to see and hear the resemblance to the blues from the seventeen-measure saxophone melody that opens the arrangement, with its disjunct, angular shape and offbeat accents. Following this statement of the head melody, the tempo shifts suddenly from the frenetic "fast" to a "slow swing" that uses a repeating $\hat{1}$-$\flat\hat{7}$ ostinato in the bass to create a bluesy feel, providing a foundation for saxophone and flute improvisation. Yet in the background of this slow section are dark, dissonant sustained chords and accents creating agitation and uncertainty. A sudden (and brief) return to the opening fast tempo and unison saxophone line brings the piece to a surprising close.

Webster had a long history together, beginning in the 1930s when both were members of Andy Kirk's Clouds of Joy. They were romantically involved for a time, and remained on friendly terms (Kernodle, *Soul on Soul*, 79; Dahl, *Morning Glory*, 92–94).

109. The 1940 recording, from June 25, first appeared as Decca 3293, and was reissued on compact disc in 1992 as Classics 640.

110. Williams's compositions from the 1960s and 1970s such as *Chief Natoma from Tacoma*, *Medi II*, *Shafi*, *Rosa Mae*, *Gloria*, *Chunka Lunka*, and others all exhibit the use of an extended bass ostinato for a significant portion of the composition. This approach can be traced in her music as far back as *Scorpio* (1946) or perhaps even to the repeated bass lines inherent in boogie-woogie (e.g., *Little Joe from Chicago*, 1937). Abrupt tempo changes such as those in *Aries Mood* and *Gravel (Truth)* can also be found in a composition like *Shafi*, from the 1970s.

Example 14.   Transformation of *Scratchin' in the Gravel* into *Gravel (Truth)* (excerpt)

Scratchin' in the Gravel, 1940 version (transcription)

Gravel (Truth), 1967 version, B1/1–4 (extracted from manuscript based on this edition)

These examples demonstrate that Williams had retained her level of comfort and familiarity with big band writing despite the more than fifteen years that had passed since she had last written for such an ensemble. Indeed, in the music of this later period she exhibits a freedom and creativity that had characterized her compositions throughout her career. Supported by an artist-in-residence position at Duke University that she accepted in 1977, Williams also wrote for various university jazz ensembles in addition to her arrangements for Herman, Basie, Ellington, and the Danish Jazz Radio Orchestra during this period. The residency, which was to last for the rest of her life, provided an economic stability that was unfamiliar to Williams. No longer obligated to seek out composing opportunities as a way of paying her bills, she could now focus on composing, performing, and teaching as duties of her academic position. Though two arrangements of her compositions stand out (*Shafi* from 1977 and *Medi II* from

Theodore E. Buehrer

Example 15.   *Aries Mood*, opening melody and "slow swing" groove (Intro/1–17, X/1–2, A1/1–10)

1978), many of her efforts were simplified to reflect the performing limitations of student ensembles, and do not represent the fullness of her later style as the other examples do.

In late 1978 Williams was diagnosed with bladder cancer. While at first the disease and its treatment did not seem to slow her down, by early 1980 the cancer had spread, and by early 1981 she was no longer able to teach her classes at Duke University. Mary Lou Williams passed away in Durham, North Carolina, on 28 May 1981.

Williams was eulogized in glowing terms. The Associated Press called her "one of the great women of jazz music for more than half a century."[111] In the *New York Times*, John S. Wilson described her as "an important contributor to every aspect of jazz that developed during a career that began in the late 1920s and lasted for more than half a century."[112] And Melvin Maddocks reflected on her piano style: "Receptive to new ideas, unfailingly generous toward other musicians, Mary Lou Williams changed as jazz changed, as though she were the persona of the jazz piano's next chorus."[113] While her role as a composer and arranger of big band music was mentioned, greater attention was placed on Williams's piano style. In fact, obituaries published at the time paid relatively little heed to her contributions as a composer of big band music. Yet taken as a whole, Williams's oeuvre in this area embodies the evolution of a style demonstrating a keen ability to bring together the various influences that swirled around her—a style, in fact, that was both personal and constantly changing. Williams also showed a willingness to move beyond conventional boundaries (of form, instrumentation, and harmony, among other things) when staying within those boundaries meant sacrificing her own artistic impulses. As her style evolved, her compositions never lost their ability to communicate with the musicians who played them or the audiences that heard them; they embodied the phenomenon of swing. Jazz writer Barry Ulanov is said to have attributed this fact to her uncanny ability to express the feeling of jazz through notation, matched only by her friend and peer Duke Ellington.[114]

Williams's works are replete with illustrations of this point, but none are more exquisite than the shout chorus of her *Walkin' and Swingin'* from 1936. Example 16 presents just the first half of this chorus, extracted from the critical edition and presented in reduced score format with annotation. The passage exhibits "the feeling of jazz" on many different levels. Here, in a swing arrangement from the 1930s, Williams combines four different riffs using contrasting instrument combinations while maintaining an infectious swing groove.[115] Starting with a figure played by saxophones and brass in block chordal (homophonic) texture, Williams then juxtaposes this riff (maintained in the saxophones) against a punched, off-beat "grunt" riff played by the brass in octaves. A call and response ensues, with similarly homophonic saxophone and brass calls answered by unison saxophones three times, the third in truncated fashion, interrupted by a culminating homophonic saxophone-and-brass gesture. The varied articulations, from short, clipped staccato notes to long accents, contribute to the passage's momentum and drive. All of this takes place against a rhythm section that provides a consistent, four-beat driving swing—the first extended passage of four-beat swing in the arrangement, which to this point has mostly followed a two-beat rhythm. This shout chorus "feels good" every time it is played or heard because its varied elements are masterfully combined. Yet it is easy to lose sight of two other subtleties. First, as Williams ends the piano solo that introduces this chorus (which she plays on all existing recordings, and would no doubt have played on the bandstand), she improvises the

---

111. "Jazz Pianist Mary Lou Williams Dead at 71."

112. Wilson, "Mary Lou Williams: A Jazz Great, Dies."

113. Maddocks, "A Celebrant of Jazz."

114. Barry Ulanov, quoted in Dahl, *Morning Glory*, 99: "One of the difficulties about jazz is that it's very hard to notate it, but Duke Ellington could and so could Mary. Very few other people have been able to put on paper the feeling of jazz . . . She has discovered, because of her particular genius, a way to articulate on paper a jazz pattern—how to accent a measure. And that's why her best stuff is among the best in jazz."

115. In the terminology that follows here and in the accompanying figure I am indebted to jazz scholar Andrew Homzy, who coined the terms "chicken" and "grunt" riffs in his presentation "*Walkin' and Swingin'*: An Examination of the Musical Structure and Performance of Mary Lou Williams' First Masterwork" at *Kool Knowledge: A Mary Lou Williams Conference* at which we were both presenters, November 16, 2002, Institute of Jazz Studies, Rutgers University-Newark. Though the terminology is inspired by his work, the analysis is my own.

Theodore E. Buehrer

Example 16. Annotated shout chorus of *Walkin' and Swingin'*

end of her solo by referencing the riff heard two bars later in the brass as the shout chorus is launched.[116] Second, while most shout choruses present new melodic and rhythmic ideas over an unaltered chord progression and formal structure, Williams bends this chorus's opening phrase to her particular purposes, making a six-measure phrase out of an eight-measure phrase. Yet her pacing of ideas here makes the formal deviation almost imperceptible. Thus, to borrow from Ulanov, this passage represents some of Williams's "best stuff," and its creativity is consistent with her big band writing overall, a body of work that transcends the imitation of styles and shows true innovation from a consummate, if unsung, artist.

---

116. As no written source for this arrangement survives, it is not known whether Williams indicated this piano figure at the end of the solo.

Theodore E. Buehrer

APPARATUS

This volume contains critically edited transcriptions and critically edited manuscripts of eleven of Williams's more than 200 big band arrangements. Chosen from throughout her career, the contents begin with *Mess-a-Stomp* (1929) and end with *Aries Mood* (1968). While a selection of works can provide only a partial view of the whole, examples chosen from across several decades of her involvement with the big band can at least trace the path of her development as a composer for this medium. An alternative approach would have been to concentrate on a shorter period of her big band work. But because jazz styles changed considerably during her long career, and Williams found a way to sound up to date in all of them, that trait seemed the right theme for a one-volume representation of her work as a big band composer and arranger.

Any anthology represents an editor's choices, and mine were influenced by a number of different criteria. If an ever-evolving compositional style is the salient feature of Williams's music that led me to include works written over a span of almost forty years, the question of how and why individual pieces were chosen remains. One guiding principle was to select works that Williams composed or co-composed. Though arrangements of others' compositions far outnumber Williams's arrangements of originals, I have chosen to restrict my choices to the latter because her own work illustrates most fully the development of her personal style. In a sense, the resulting arrangements are "purely Williams," unfettered by the constraints of someone else's song or arrangement of that song. This decision narrowed my choices from over 200 arrangements for big band to fewer than fifty. A second principle was to select, as much as possible, compositions for which reliable autograph sources were extant. Such sources provide an authoritative weight and accuracy to the music presented here that, for example, a volume consisting entirely of aural transcriptions could not, given the complexities and difficulties inherent in the transcription process, especially when it involves multilayered ensemble music recorded with the limited technology available during the early stages of the composer's career. Yet, since no written sources of Williams's music are known to exist from before 1937, this principle was overridden in three cases (*Mess-a-Stomp*, 1929; *Mary's Idea*, 1930; and *Walkin' and Swingin'*, 1936) so that the volume could represent the entire range of Williams's styles. And it was set aside in a fourth instance (*In the Land of Oo-Bla-Dee*, 1949) to provide an example of Williams's breadth and flexibility, which allowed a lighthearted novelty number in the form of a popular song for a band led by a pioneer of modern jazz. In the end, of the eleven compositions in this volume, seven are based on written musical sources, while the remaining four are my own transcriptions from recordings.

New arrangements of music that Williams had composed earlier were another factor in choosing the contents of this volume. During the late 1930s especially, Williams drew from works she had arranged as her earliest efforts, beginning in 1929. To compare treatments of the same composition over a time span of almost a decade is another way of measuring how her style evolved. Thus, the volume contains two versions of *Mess-a-Stomp* (1929 and 1938, the latter retitled *Messa Stomp*) and of *Mary's Idea* (1930 and 1938). Another principle (already noted) was to represent the variety of Williams's works—from *In the Land of Oo-Bla-Dee* (1949) for Dizzy Gillespie's band, to *Scorpio* (1946) for Duke Ellington's, to *Aries Mood* (1968). The latter two pieces differ as much from each other, and from Williams's work in the 1930s and early 1940s, as can be imagined. But with her, variety takes many forms. I wished also to convey the respect Williams's music commanded from other bandleaders. Her ability to provide music suited to the style of the band for which she was writing helps to explain that respect. I also sought to represent the variety of styles swirling around Williams and her ability to include something of that variety in her music: from the blues influences of late-1920s Kansas City to the swing of the 1930s, from the modernist and bebop influences of 1940s New York to the harmonic complexity and experimentation of the 1960s. And last, I wished to highlight, in at least a couple of examples, Williams's prowess as an improviser at the piano, and how these abilities were woven into the big band arrangements of her works.

Guiding these decisions was my determination to represent the artistic quality of Williams's work: her desire to push beyond conventional style and genre boundaries and explore creative solutions that succeed in maintaining a swing feel and a listener's interest.

This volume is the first to present a selection of Mary Lou Williams's big band compositions in the form of a critical edition. Some of the compositions included here have already been published in one form or another. A section "Musical Scores" in the bibliography lists a selection of these publications. Care must be taken, however, to assess which written version or recorded take provides the source of these publications, and how reliable the editorial method has been. This volume, for example, publishes for the first time an edition of the 1938 manuscript version of *Messa Stomp* and of the manuscripts of *Gravel (Truth)* (1967) and *Aries Mood* (1968). Each score is introduced with data about its sources, the history of the tune represented, and a brief commentary describing salient features of the arrangement. Critical notes follow each score.

Sources and Editorial Methods

Scores

A variety of sources and editorial methods stands behind this volume. Seven of the eleven arrangements are based on written source material. Many of Williams's scores and parts survive and are catalogued in the Mary Lou Williams Collection at the Institute of Jazz Studies at Rutgers University-Newark (New Jersey).[1] Additional scores (and parts) by Williams survive in other archival collections, most notably the Duke Ellington Collection in the Archives Center at the Smithsonian Museum of

---

1. The Mary Lou Williams Collection was donated to the Institute of Jazz Studies in 1999 by Peter O'Brien, Executive Director of the Mary Lou Williams Foundation. The collection is large, and it is substantial. Williams left behind a vast body of work, including over 200 original compositions, many more arrangements, and over 150 recordings (commercial CDs, LPs, and 78s, as well as unissued tapes). The collection contains approximately 170 cubic feet of Williams's musical scores, sound recordings, personal papers, scrapbooks, photographs, videotapes, and books. With the help of a grant from the National Endowment for the Humanities, cataloguing of the collection was completed in November of 2002.

Theodore E. Buehrer

American History and the Benny Goodman Papers at Yale University. The existence of many full scores of Williams's works invites close study of her compositional processes and development over time. I have made many trips to these archives, most notably the Mary Lou Williams Collection, and I have acquired copies of scores (both complete and incomplete), sketches (from loose-leaf pages and from sketchbooks), and parts for each of the arrangements. I worked from scores and sketches in Williams's own hand whenever possible, and checked these against sets of parts (complete or incomplete) where parts exist. One score was chosen as the primary source, with other score variants, parts, and sketches serving as secondary sources throughout this project. Where both written and aural sources existed for the same composition, written sources received preferential treatment over recordings. Major discrepancies between primary sources (scores) and these alternative sources (audio recordings) are referred to in a separate section of the critical notes when it seemed appropriate, but I gave preference to the primary source(s) in my edited score. I have been influenced in this decision by the relatively recent publication of Miles Davis's *Birth of the Cool* scores, edited by Jeff Sultanof.[2] Though Sultanof's work does not constitute a critical edition in the manner outlined here (i.e., the scores are not accompanied by critical annotations, nor are the editorial methods explained), his decision to remain faithful to the scores and parts in his edition, even when the recording points in a different direction, is sound and worthy of emulating in this work.

Transcriptions from Recordings

Many of Williams's arrangements have no surviving score or parts, including nearly all of the arrangements she prepared for Andy Kirk's band.[3] The Mary Lou Williams Collection holds many transcriptions from recordings of her works; these transcriptions were created within the last twenty years primarily for the purpose of performing these works at tribute or dedicatory concerts. All four of the transcribed scores in this volume (*Mess-a-Stomp*, 1929; *Mary's Idea*, 1930; *Walkin' and Swingin'*, 1936; and *In the Land of Oo-Bla-Dee*, 1949), however, are my own, and where applicable, they were compared to existing transcriptions as a check.[4] These four scores, therefore, rely solely on the recording cited for each of these tunes. As argued in other volumes in the MUSA series, particularly by Paul S. Machlin in his volume on Fats Waller and by Jeffrey Taylor in his volume on Earl Hines, transcriptions of recorded music are at best approximations of what actually occurred in the recorded performance.[5] In the cases of Waller and Hines, the transcriptions provide notation of what was primarily (if not exclusively) improvised music. In the case of Williams's arrangements, I provide notation of what was primarily written-out music. Thus, my transcriptions amount to documents that, as Machlin asserts in his volume, are both *descriptive* of what Williams likely intended in her arrangement and *prescriptive* should others wish to duplicate these performances.[6] My transcriptions were made through close, repeated listenings, using a computer software tool called *Transcribe!* on an ad hoc (but frequent) basis. Using mp3-formatted versions of the audio recordings, this program not only allowed

---

2. See Davis, *Birth of the Cool*.

3. The most likely explanation for this void in the Mary Lou Williams Collection is that Williams left Kirk's band on poor terms, and did not claim scores of hers that were surely in Kirk's possession. The present location of the Kirk band's book is unknown (according to private correspondence with Peter O'Brien, Williams's last manager and Executive Director of the Mary Lou Williams Foundation).

4. For all four of these works, the Mary Lou Williams Collection contains transcriptions by Mark Lopeman, c. 2000. For *Walkin' and Swingin'* the collection also includes a transcription by Ricky Ford, date unknown.

5. Waller, *Performances in Transcription*; Hines, *Selected Piano Solos*.

6. Waller, 192–93.

me to slow down audio files in order to hear and understand a passage more clearly, but it also provided a graphic representation of the audio as a waveform, and allowed me to highlight any portion of the waveform (e.g., a chord or short melodic fragment), on which *Transcribe!* would then perform a frequency analysis and map its results onto a virtual piano keyboard. Additionally, *Transcribe!*'s built-in equalization (EQ) filtering tools allowed me to focus in on particular frequency bands of an audio file while reducing (or eliminating) others, enabling me to listen closely to inner or lower parts without the distraction of higher, more melodic parts. Despite the power of this tool, *Transcribe!* did not do the work of transcription for me. I relied on my ear, a nearby MIDI keyboard used to play and experiment with what I thought I was hearing in the recordings, and musical intuitions honed over some twenty years of working with and playing jazz music. Still, hearing every pitch played by every individual instrument, particularly in the thickest, most densely textured passages, was an extremely difficult task.

Notation

The editions in this volume follow standard Western musical convention and contain the varied kinds of musical notation one would expect to find in jazz scores. Editorial musical markings and accidentals are indicated by brackets or parentheses or, in the case of slurs and hairpins, are represented with dashed lines. If a marking has been changed, an additional critical note indicates the reading of the primary source. If no critical note is provided, the editorial marking was added for consistency. Corrections of pitch levels are indicated in the critical notes only.

ACCIDENTALS

Accidentals introduced into the score are canceled at the end of the measure by the barline; on occasion, a courtesy repetition or cancellation may appear in parentheses. Courtesy accidentals are added without report in the critical notes.

ENHARMONIC SPELLINGS

I have maintained Williams's sometimes idiosyncratic enharmonic spellings of pitches, even when they obscure a pitch's function in a chord. For example, if in a passage governed by an A7 harmony, Williams writes a pitch as D♭, I have written the pitch exactly as she did, even though its enharmonic spelling, C♯, helps us to better understand the pitch's role as the 3rd of the chord.

REPEAT MARKINGS

Shortcut repeat marks are realized without further notice in the critical notes. Longer instructions like "Copy 4 of A" are mentioned, however.

SLASH NOTATION

Each chord symbol accompanied by a corresponding number of slash marks (usually two or four, but sometimes more) indicates that a particular harmony is to be played (guitar or piano), outlined (bass), or soloed over (any instrument) in an improvised fashion until the next chord symbol is reached, at which point *that* harmony is to be realized. Generally, a slash is assumed to receive the rhythmic value of the basic beat. At other times (particularly for rhythm section instruments), slashes have rhythmic values attached to them, indicating a specific rhythm in which the chord or chords are to be played.

DRUM NOTATION

Drum notation presents another special case. In the four arrangements based on aural transcriptions (no written sources being available), I transcribed everything, including the drum part, and provided notation in the drum line following conventions established by Norman Weinberg in his *Guide to Standardized Drumset Notation*, published by the Percussive Arts Society (1998). Under these conventions, each individual drum, cymbal, or other percussive instrument is assigned a corresponding line or space in the staff and each its own notehead shape. In the other seven arrangements, on which I worked from written sources, I wrote whatever drum notation was provided in the scores and/or parts. Sometimes this notation follows Weinberg's conventions, but sometimes it does not. Slash notation is common in drum parts, then and now, and simply means for the drummer to provide basic swing rhythmic feel on the drum set. But some of Williams's drum notation consists merely of an instruction at the beginning of a section followed by rests (or empty measures) for the entire section (e.g., "16 Swing"). Such a marking tells the drummer to play a swing rhythm for sixteen measures. This was a standard method of quickly providing instruction and direction for the drummer. In these cases, I provide slash notation, which has become more conventional, through these passages.

Improvised Solos

As noted, in the four aurally transcribed scores I transcribed everything, including all improvised solos for piano and other instruments. In the other seven scores, working from written sources, I included solos only when Williams herself notated them in the primary source. Most of the time, however, she left the staff blank, and in all but one of these cases I provided slash markings and chord symbols. *Messa Stomp* (1938) was the exception, for here I included the piano solo that Williams herself played on the recording. It is my belief that, in a critical edition of Williams's music, a sample of how she improvised on one her own compositions carries aesthetic, historical, and even pedagogical weight.

Chord Nomenclature

The method of notating chord sonorities in jazz writing is not an entirely standard process. Just as the system for labeling chords with Roman numerals has variations (e.g., all uppercase, as opposed to using upper- and lowercase to distinguish major from minor mode), chord sonorities used in jazz may be indicated with slightly different symbols. Convention has it that chord symbols appear above the staves to which they refer. Generally they include the root name and (in most cases) some identifying symbol. Throughout this volume, the symbols that appear are those that Williams herself used. In the case of the four aural transcriptions, I have adopted a consistent method of labeling using the chord symbols most commonly used today. The basic chord sonorities found throughout this edition are summarized in Table 1 below. Where variants are common, these are indicated as well.

Chord extensions may be combined in symbols describing more complex chords. For example, $D^{7\flat 5}_{\flat 9}$ describes a dominant 7th chord on D with a lowered 5th and lowered 9th (D-F♯-A♭-C-E♭). Dominant chords may sometimes be modified by including two chromatically altered extensions. Typically, these two will be chosen from either (a) the lowered 5th (raised 11th) or raised 5th (lowered 13th), but not both; or (b) the lowered 9th or raised 9th, but not both. Such chords are called "altered chords," abbreviated "alt." For example, D7alt describes a dominant 7th chord that might contain a lowered 5th and lowered 9th, as described above, but it might instead contain a raised 5th (lowered 13th) and raised 9th.[7]

A related issue concerns enharmonic spelling of chords and the use of enharmonic notes in melodies. Training in the tradition of Western art music teaches that note spelling should coincide with chord function as much as possible, and therefore a D7

---

7. For more information on "alt" chords, see Levine, *The Jazz Theory Book*, Chapter 3.

Table 1.   Basic chord sonorities

Chord Type	Symbol	Example	Spelling	Variants
Major triad	Root name	D	D-F♯-A	DM
Minor triad	Root name & lowercase "m"	Dm	D-F-A	D-
Diminished triad	Root name & "o"	D°	D-F-A♭	Ddim
Augmented triad	Root name & "+"	D+	D-F♯-A♯	Daug
Major add6	Root name & "6"	D6	D-F♯-A-B	D$^{6/9}$
Major 7th	Root name & "maj7"	Dmaj7	D-F♯-A-C♯	Dma7, D^{M7}, D$^{\Delta}$, D$^{\Delta7}$
Dominant 7th	Root name & "7"	D7	D-F♯-A-C	
Minor 7th	Root name & "m7"	Dm7	D-F-A-C	D-7
Minor-major 7th	Root name & "m^{maj7}"	Dm^{maj7}	D-F-A-C♯	Dm$^{\Delta7}$, Dm7+
Half-diminished 7th	Root name & "m7♭5"	Dm7♭5	D-F-A♭-C	D$^{\varnothing7}$, Dm7-5
Fully-diminished 7th	Root name & "o7"	D^{o7}	D-F-A♭-C♭	Ddim7
Dominant 7th ♯5	Root name & "+7"	D^{+7}	D-F♯-A♯-C	D7♯5, D7+5
Dominant 9th	Root name & "9"	D9	D-F♯-A-C-E	
Dominant ♭9th	Root name & "7♭9"	D7♭9	D-F♯-A-C-E♭	D7-9
Dominant ♯9th	Root name & "7♯9"	D7♯9	D-F♯-A-C-E♯	D7+9
Major 9th	Root name & "maj9"	Dmaj9	D-F♯-A-C♯-E	Dma9, D^{M9}, D$^{\Delta9}$
Minor 9th	Root name & "m9"	Dm9	D-F-A-C-E	D-9

should be spelled D-F♯-A-C, never D-G♭-A-C. Williams's approach to enharmonicism (and, indeed, the approach that can be observed in much jazz music) is much looser. Another common respelling in these editions concerns pairs of chords that possess the same pitches but that can be understood to have different roots. For example, D6 (D-F♯-A-B) and Bm7 (B-D-F♯-A) are used interchangeably in Williams's practice. Most the time she makes note and chord spelling choices consistent with prevailing harmonic function, but there are plenty of examples where an enharmonic note choice or chord spelling is made, and the reader should be aware of these inconsistencies.

MUSICAL MARKINGS

The following list provides a catalogue and brief descriptions of the various types of musical markings that can be found throughout the volume.

Accent. An articulation played with a heavy, long emphasis on the note.

Tenuto. An articulation played in a long, sustained fashion. Like the accent, the tenuto points to longer, full-value notes.

Marcato. An articulation played with a loud, sharp emphasis on the note. It is not as long as the accent above but louder and more heavily punctuated than the staccato below.

Staccato. An articulation played in a short, detached fashion. Both staccato and marcato suggest that the note so marked is to last less than its full written value.

Theodore E. Buehrer

Fall (or Drop). Once the notated pitch is sounded, the pitch is quickly forced downwards, usually to an indeterminate pitch, with several indeterminate pitches slurred through along the way. Different instruments achieve this effect differently: reeds with fingerings or lips; trumpets with lips, half-valves, or rapid fingering (or some combination of the three); trombones with lips and the slide; string instruments (guitar and bass) by sliding the left hand down the neck as the string continues to vibrate; piano by a fast glissando downwards.

 Bend. This marking is typically seen in horn parts. It involves establishing the pitch, then using the lips to bring the pitch down by one half step, then returning to the original pitch, all within the amount of time allowed in the given durational value. Williams used both the u-like symbol above or below a note and the instruction "Bend" (with no symbol) to indicate this technique.

 Squeeze (or Slide). This is another typical marking for horns. Its effect is to approach ("slide" into) the notated pitch from an indeterminate pitch below. The player must arrive at the notated pitch on the beat, which means that the squeeze/slide begins earlier, usually within a half beat or less. Like the drop (above), it is achieved differently by the different instruments: with fast chromatic fingerings by the reeds; a combination of lipping and half-valves with the trumpet; and the use of the slide by the trombone.

 Shake. A shake for horn players involves a (usually) fast trill between the written pitch and an indeterminate pitch above what is written, not usually more than the interval of a third above the written pitch. The shake begins immediately upon the attack of the written pitch and lasts for its rhythmic duration.

 *Glissando (Gliss).* The glissando is a fast chromatic run between two determinate pitches. Williams uses both the glissando symbol shown here and the instruction "Smear" plus a line or slur marking between two notes for the same effect.

 Grace Notes. Grace notes are played before the beat.

 Tremolo. This marking appears in transcriptions of Williams's piano solos in one of two ways (shown). Both are to be played as a rapid alternation between the two pitches for the duration indicated (in each of the examples, two beats).

Plunger

 Plunger. Williams's scores call for the use of the plunger mute (a standard plumber's plunger with the handle removed) in several places. Brass players would hold the plunger in front of the instrument's bell and move it according to the + and o markings above the affected notes. The + means the plunger should cover the bell enough to muffle the sound. The o means that the plunger should be removed from the bell so that the instrument can produce its normal sound.

 Slurs. Slurs are used throughout to indicate legato articulation between the notes, or to indicate phrasing, or both. Sometimes Williams does not apply the slur marking, but writes out the word "slur." In these cases the edition replaces the word with the marking silently and reports only the first occurrence of such substitution in each composition in the critical notes.

Ad lib. This term means that the instrument to which it refers is to improvise, using the governing chords (symbols typically provided) to guide note choices. It does not mean that the performer can choose whether or not to play the part in question (as the term may be used in other musical contexts).

Derby (or Hat). This marking applies to brass instruments, and involves the use of a Derby hat placed in front of the instrument's bell (similarly to the plunger, above). The result is a slightly muffled, darker timbre than normal. Occasionally the + and o symbols are used in conjunction with the Derby hat to indicate the hat's placement relative to the instrument's bell (as with the plunger). If these symbols are not used, the assumption is that the hat should cover the bell (again, allowing some room for sound to project).

Dynamics

In the seven compositions edited from written sources, editorial changes of dynamic markings are indicated by brackets and a report in the critical notes if necessary. In the four scores created by aural transcription, the dynamics have been determined by the editor based on the nuances heard in the recordings.

Rhythms

Following jazz notational convention, Williams writes all of her eighth notes without differentiation, even though in practice she means them to be swung eighth notes, whereby the first eighth note of a two-note grouping is longer than the second (by a ratio of approximately 2:1). Thus, throughout the volume, unless otherwise indicated:

♫ = ♩♪ and ♫ = ♪♩

Critical Commentary

The reader interested in discrepancies between sources, errors found in sources, and interpretive or other similar issues should have the critical notes handy when studying any of the scores. Following the precedent set in three earlier MUSA editions of jazz music (Paul Machlin's edition of Fats Waller transcriptions, Jeffrey Taylor's edition of Earl Hines transcriptions, and John J. Joyce Jr., Bruce Boyd Raeburn, and Anthony M. Cummings's edition of Sam Morgan's Jazz Band transcriptions), all critical notes for a score have been placed immediately following that music.[8]

Pitches are cited in the critical notes at their written levels and according to the Helmholtz method of pitch notation, where "middle C" is labeled as c′, the octave

---

8. Waller, *Performances in Transcription*; Hines, *Selected Piano Solos*; and Sam Morgan's Jazz Band, *Complete Recorded Works in Transcription.*

below that as c, below that as C, and below that as C_1. Above "middle C," the next octave is labeled c″, and subsequent octaves are designated accordingly.

Abbreviations used for instruments in the critical notes include: ASax = alto saxophone, B = bass, Ban = banjo, BSax = baritone saxophone, Cl = clarinet, Dr = drums, Gtr = guitar, Pn = piano, Tb = tuba, Tpt = trumpet, Trb = trombone, TSax = tenor saxophone, V = voice, and Vn = violin.

Abbreviations used for collections referred to in the critical notes include: MLWC = Mary Lou Williams Collection, Institute of Jazz Studies, Rutgers University, Newark, NJ; BGP = Benny Goodman Papers, Irving S. Gilmore Music Library, Yale University, New Haven, CT; and DEC = Duke Ellington Collection, Smithsonian National Museum of American History Archives Center, Washington, D.C.

The critical notes apply to points in the scores where an editorial decision was made or a commentary needed. They describe the finding in the primary source and provide an explanation for the editorial decision if one is needed. These points are indicated mostly by section marker(s), measure number(s) within that section, and the number(s) of the rhythmic notational element(s)—counting only noteheads and rests, from left to right—within the measure. For example, the entry "A2/12.1–2, Tpt 1, Trb 3: 'slur' indicated; not applied here as tone repetitions are being played" refers to the first and second rhythmic elements in the Trumpet 1 and Trombone 3 parts of measure 12 in section A2. For these rhythmic elements, in this case actual pitches and not rests, Williams writes the indication "slur." Because the two pitches are tone repetitions, this indication was not applied here, meaning in this edition.

Plate 1. *Messa Stomp* (1938) autograph, Intro/1–4 and A1/1–4. The Mary Lou Williams Collection, Institute of Jazz Studies, Rutgers University-Newark; used by permission.

Plate 1 continued.

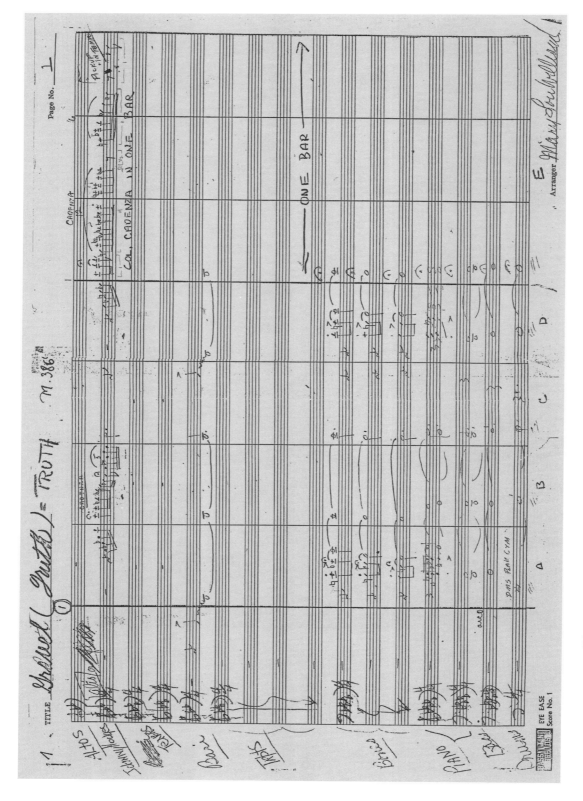

Plate 2. *Gravel (Truth)* (1967) autograph, Intro/1–5. The Mary Lou Williams Collection, Institute of Jazz Studies, Rutgers University-Newark; used by permission.

SELECTED WORKS FOR BIG BAND

MESS-A-STOMP (1929)

For Andy Kirk. Transcription From Recording

Composer.   Mary Lou Williams

Primary Source.   Recording: Brunswick 4694, matrix KC-591-, reissued as Classics Records, Classics 655 (compact disc, 1992)

Date of Composition.   Uncertain; probably 1929

Date and Location of Recording.   C. 7 November 1929, Kansas City, MO, Radio Station KMBC

Band.   Andy Kirk and His Twelve Clouds of Joy

Personnel.   Gene Prince, Harry Lawson, trumpets; Allen Durham, trombone; John Harrington, clarinet/alto saxophone; John Williams, alto saxophone; Lawrence Freeman, tenor saxophone; Mary Lou Williams, piano; William Dirvin, banjo/guitar; Claude Williams, solo guitar; Andy Kirk, brass bass (tuba), leader; Edward McNeil, drums

Form.   Key B♭: Intro$_{(4)}$ A1$_{(Cl, 12)}$ A2$_{(Cl,12)}$ Key Gm: X$_{(4)}$ B1$_{(Saxes, 8)}$ B2$_{(Saxes, Tpt 8)}$ Key B♭: A3$_{(Pn, 12)}$ A4$_{(Pn, 12)}$ C1$_{(Brass, 12)}$ C2$_{(Brass, 12)}$ A5$_{(Gtr, Ban, 13)}$ A6$_{(12)}$ Tag$_{(4)}$

*M*ess-a-Stomp is one of Mary Lou Williams's earliest compositions and her first arrangement for big band. Its recording in November 1929 took place at the Clouds of Joy's first recording session. Reflecting the largely improvised nature of Kansas City big band arrangements at the time, *Mess-a-Stomp* provides ample room for improvised melody, with the clarinet playing two blues choruses at the opening, and trumpet, piano, and banjo also receiving solo space. At the same time, Williams balances solo improvising with arranged passages for harmonized horns. In this arrangement a repeated eight-bar B strain is interjected into a succession of twelve-bar blues choruses (labeled "A" in the formal chart), demonstrating the young Williams's handling of multi-strained popular music of that time. Her two-chorus piano solo (transcribed in the edition from the recording) also shows her mastery of the stride piano style, with its rhythmically solid left hand providing harmonic support as her right hand plays a more complicated syncopated melody.

MESS-A-STOMP
(1 9 2 9)

Mary Lou Williams

MESS-A-STOMP (1929)

Mary Lou Williams

Mary Lou Williams

Mary Lou Williams

Mary Lou Williams

Mary Lou Williams

MESS-A-STOMP (1929)

A5

Mary Lou Williams

Mary Lou Williams

Mary Lou Williams

CRITICAL COMMENTARY

Though William Dirvin is listed as the band's banjo *and* guitar player in both the CD liner notes and Brian Rust's *Jazz Records: 1897–1942*, both instruments are clearly heard playing simultaneously during the guitar solo, A5/1–11.1. The discography compiled by Howard Rye and published as an appendix of Andy Kirk's autobiography, *Twenty Years on Wheels*, clarifies this situation by identifying Claude Williams as the solo guitarist. I have included staves for both Banjo and Guitar in the edition, even though this brief passage is the only place that both instruments are heard.

Critical Notes

B2/7.1, Tpt 1: pitch of "fluffed" note is hard to discern; solution is conjectural.
B2/8–A4/12, Pn: improvisation by Williams.
A3/12.2–4, Pn (RH, LH): not fully audible; solution is conjectural.
A4/4.3, Pn (RH): g‴ accidentally struck with f♯‴; removed for clarity.
A4/4.4, Pn (RH): f‴ accidentally struck with g‴; removed for clarity.
A6/6.2, Tpt 2: d″ accidentally played; f″ suggested.
A6/7–8, Trb: inaudible, possibly tacet, but unlikely; solution is conjectural.
A6/9.2, Tpt 1: g″ accidentally played; a″ suggested.

Mary Lou Williams

MARY'S IDEA (1930)

For Andy Kirk. Transcription from Recording

Composer.   Mary Lou Williams

Primary Source.   Recording: Brunswick 4863, matrix C-4473-A, reissued as Classics Records, Classics 655 (compact disc, 1992)

Date of Composition.   Uncertain; probably 1930

Date and Location of Recording.   1 May 1930, Chicago, IL

Band.   Andy Kirk and His Twelve Clouds of Joy

Personnel.   Edgar Battle, Harry Lawson, trumpets; Allen Durham, trombone; John Harrington, clarinet/alto saxophone; John Williams, alto saxophone/baritone saxophone; Lawrence Freeman, tenor saxophone; Mary Lou Williams, piano; William Dirvin, banjo; Andy Kirk, brass bass (tuba), leader; Edward McNeil, drums

Form.   Key E♭: Intro$_{(10)}$ A1$_{(Tpt, 8+8+8+8=32)}$ A2$_{(BSax, 8+8+8+8=32)}$ X$_{(6+8+8=22)}$ A3$_{(Cl, ASax, 8+8+8+8=32)}$ A4$_{(8+8+8+6=30)}$ Tag$_{(4)}$

Like *Mess-a-Stomp* (1929), this arrangement of *Mary's Idea* is another example of Williams's earliest composing and arranging work. Recorded on the last of a three-day session in late April/early May 1930 in Chicago, this piece comes from the second recording session of Kirk's Clouds of Joy. *Mary's Idea* is a thirty-two-bar *aaba* structure that continues the emphasis on improvised melodies (trumpet, baritone saxophone, clarinet, and alto saxophone are all given solo opportunities) while also containing tightly arranged ensemble writing that sometimes backs the soloists and at other times is more prominent. At the end of the piece, the final *a* section of A4 is shortened to six bars to make room for a four-bar ending tag that incorporates a rhythmically disorienting device known as back-beating, borrowed from stride piano. In particular, Williams has the tuba disrupt the regular accented note on beats 1 and 3 and uses the other horns to provide mid-register chord punches in a way that mimics the left-hand stride piano stylings of James P. Johnson and Fats Waller, not to mention Williams herself.

MARY'S IDEA

(1 9 3 0)

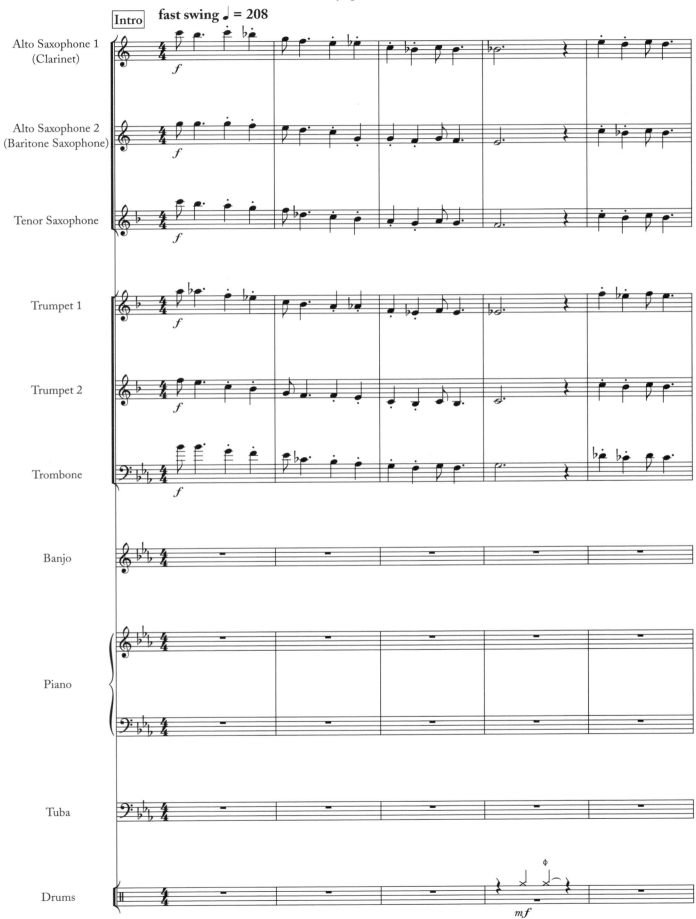

Mary Lou Williams

Mary Lou Williams

Mary Lou Williams

Mary Lou Williams

Mary Lou Williams

MARY'S IDEA (1930)

38   Mary Lou Williams

Mary Lou Williams

Mary Lou Williams

Mary Lou Williams

Mary Lou Williams

Mary Lou Williams

MARY'S IDEA (1930)

Mary Lou Williams

Mary Lou Williams

Critical Notes

Intro/5.1, Tpt 1: a″ (approximately) accidentally played.

A1/20.1, Tb: A accidentally played two beats early; suggested pitch supports Saxes' A♭ major chord voicing.

A2/18.2, Trb: a♭′; likely incorrect given Williams's preference for full triads.

A2/18.4, Trb: inaudible, but likely played.

A2/27, Trb: rhythmically dissimilar to rest of horns, likely a mistake.

X/11.1, Tpt 1: b♭″ accidentally played.

A3/3.2, ASax 2, TSax, Trb: chord voicing inaudible.

A3/3.3, Ban, Pn: chord voicing inaudible.

A3/17.2, TSax: g♭′ accidentally played.

A4/1.1–2, Trb: rhythmically dissimilar to rest of horns, likely a mistake.

A4/1.1, Tb: inaudible.

A4/12.4, Tpt 1: c‴ accidentally played; suggested pitch matches ASax 1 in 10.4.

A4/25.2–3, Trb: rhythmically dissimilar to rest of horns, likely a mistake.

WALKIN' AND SWINGIN' (1936)

For Andy Kirk. Transcription from Recording (Take C)

Composer. Mary Lou Williams

Primary Source. Recording: Decca 809, matrix 60852-C (Take C), reissued as MCA/GRP, GRD 622 (compact disc, 1993)

Date of Composition. Uncertain; probably 1936

Date and Location of Recording. 2 March 1936, New York City

Band. Andy Kirk and His Twelve Clouds of Joy

Personnel. Harry Lawson, Paul King, Earl Thompson, trumpets; Ted Donnelly, Henry Wells, trombone; John Harrington, John Williams, alto saxophones; Dick Wilson, tenor saxophone; Mary Lou Williams, piano; Ted Brinson, guitar; Booker Collins, bass; Ben Thigpen, drums

Form. Key A♭: A1$_{(8+8+8+10=34)}$ Key F: A2$_{(8+8+8+8=32)}$ A3$_{(Pn, TSax, 8+8+8+8=32)}$ A4$_{(6+8+8+8=30)}$

Because of hardships brought on by the Great Depression, *Walkin' and Swingin'* was the first recording made by Andy Kirk and His Clouds of Joy in five years. The composition measures the maturing of Mary Lou Williams's style during that period. The band's size had grown, particularly in the brass section, yet the music's feel remains light and uncluttered. In the second chorus (A2) Williams comes up with an inventive orchestration of a lead trumpet harmonized by three saxophones. About this passage she later observed that "I needed a fourth saxophone but during that period you had only three. As I didn't have a fourth, I used a trumpet . . . for the eighth notes. This was an innovation for the time; the musicians loved it."[1] A melodic fragment is heard in the last eight measures of A2 that would later become part of Thelonious Monk's tune *Rhythm-a-Ning* (1957). Williams's role as a mentor to Monk in the 1940s, mentioned in the essay above, may explain his apparent borrowing from a number she had written almost two decades earlier.[2]

---

1. Dahl, *Morning Glory*, 94. The quote is from an interview Williams gave on KUON, Nebraska Educational Television in 1980. See pp. xxxii, xxxiv–xxxv.

2. Monk's *Rhythm-a-Ning* belongs to the family of so-called "rhythm changes" tunes based on the harmonic structure of George Gershwin's *I Got Rhythm*. Williams's *Walkin' and Swingin'*, however, cannot be included in that family. Although it shares the repeated I-VI-II-V progression in the first four measures of each eight-bar *a* section, a standard trait of "rhythm changes" tunes, it diverges harmonically in each *a* section's second phrase, and also in the bridge (*b*). Monk's apparent borrowing from Williams may have been indirect, for according to Robin D. G. Kelley in *Thelonious Monk*, 74, in 1941 guitarist Charlie Christian recorded a song titled *Meet Dr. Christian* containing an eight-bar opening that seems to have been taken almost verbatim from this passage of *Walkin' and Swingin'*, a point verified by Chris Sheridan in *Brilliant Corners*, 5. For more on the origins of the "rhythm changes" tunes see Crawford, *American Musical Landscape*, Chapter 7.

Although recorded on the same date, two recordings of this work (matrix 60852-A and 60852-C, respectively) offer different representations of the piece.[3] Take A has a tempo of ♩ = 178, while Take C's tempo is closer to ♩ = 194. Additionally, the rhythm section instruments (Gtr, Pn, B, and Dr) do not play exactly the same rhythms, lines, chords, etc., because a lot of these parts were improvised. Other discrepancies between Take C and Take A are documented in the Critical Notes section. Take C was chosen to be transcribed here primarily because of the quality of Williams's piano solo and the perfect way her final gesture (A3/29–30) anticipates the unison horn call that follows (A3/31–32).

From a formal standpoint, the basic structure of the composition is thirty-two-bar *aaba*, repeated for a total of four choruses. However, Williams manipulates this form twice to fit her compositional purposes: in A1, she lengthens the final section from eight to ten measures for transition to the new key in A2. And in A4, she truncates the first section from eight to six measures, starting a new melodic/rhythmic figure at A4/7 that coincides with the beginning of the second phrase.

---

3. *Take A:* Columbia (E) DB5023, matrix 60852-A, recorded 2 March 1936, New York City, reissued as Classics Records, Classics 573 (CD) in 1991.

WALKIN' AND SWINGIN'
(1 9 3 6)

Mary Lou Williams

Mary Lou Williams

Walkin' and Swingin' (1936)

Mary Lou Williams

WALKIN' AND SWINGIN' (1936)

64   Mary Lou Williams

Mary Lou Williams

WALKIN' AND SWINGIN' (1936)

Mary Lou Williams

Mary Lou Williams

Mary Lou Williams

Mary Lou Williams

Mary Lou Williams

WALKIN' AND SWINGIN' (1936)

Mary Lou Williams

Mary Lou Williams

WALKIN' AND SWINGIN' (1936)

CRITICAL COMMENTARY

Critical Notes

A1/1, Brass: muffled tone quality on recording could also be created by Derby hat.

A1/19.6, Tpt 3: a′ accidentally played.

A2/9.5, Tpt 3: e♭″ accidentally played.

A2/11.5, Tpt 3: e♭″ accidentally played.

A2/16.6, Saxes, Tpt 3: F6 chord clashes with A♭7 chord in rhythm section.

A2/29.2–5, Saxes, Tpt 3: recording not clear.

A3/16.2–3, Pn (LH): Williams plays dyads as "broken 10ths," rolling them from bottom to top.

Differences Found in Take A

A1/1–6, 9–14, 25–30, Tpts, Trbs: open.

A2/2.3, Tpt 3: d″ possible error.

A2/16.2, Tpt 3, Saxes: sixteenth-note upper neighbor figure breaks up four consecutive eighth notes in first two beats of measure.

A2/16.6, Tpt 3, Saxes: A♭7 chord matching the rhythm section's chord (sounding pitches: ASax 1 = c″, ASax 2 = a♭′, TSax = c″, Tpt 3 = a♭′).

A2/22.5, Tpt 3, Saxes: same chord as 22.3; possibly sloppy cutoff rather than intentionally different rhythmic figure.

A2/24.6, Tpt 3: b♭′ possible error.

A3/1–32, Pn, TSax: different improvisation.

A4/13.2–14.2, Trbs: in harmony with Saxes.

A4/15–20, Saxes, Trb 1: parts are swapped, Trb 1 on lead, then ASax 1, ASax 2, and TSax; rhythm of harmonized soli slightly different in A4/17 (syncopation into beat 2), and no glissando into A4/18, beat 2.

A4/16–19, Tpts: calls in unison.

A4/24.5, Saxes, Trb: ends with downward movement.

A MELLOW BIT OF RHYTHM (1937)

For Andy Kirk. Edited from Manuscript

Composer.   Mary Lou Williams and Herman Walder

Primary Source.   Autograph score in Williams's hand. Mary Lou Williams Collection, Institute of Jazz Studies, Rutgers University, Newark, NJ

Date of Composition.   Uncertain; probably 1937

Recording.   Decca 1579, matrix 62446-A, reissued as Classics Records, Classics 581 (compact disc, 1991)

Date and Location of Recording.   26 July 1937, New York City

Band.   Andy Kirk and His Twelve Clouds of Joy

Personnel.   Harry Lawson, Paul King, Earl Thompson, trumpets; Ted Donnelly, Henry Wells, trombones; John Harrington, clarinet/alto saxophone; Earl Miller, alto saxophone; Dick Wilson, tenor saxophone; John Williams, alto/baritone saxophones; Mary Lou Williams, piano; Ted Brinson, guitar; Booker Collins, bass; Ben Thigpen, drums

Form.   Key E♭: Intro$_{(8)}$ A1$_{(8+8+8+8=32)}$ X1$_{(8)}$ A2$_{(TSax, Tpt, 8+8+8+8=32)}$ A3$_{(Cl, 8+8+8+6=30)}$ X2$_{(4)}$ A4$_{(8+8+8+8=32)}$

This piece was co-composed by Williams and tenor saxophonist Herman Walder, though the arrangement was most likely made by Williams. Its appeal as a swing dance number is shown by the existence of arrangements provided for other bands—the Lionel Hampton Orchestra, the Benny Goodman Orchestra, and the Les Brown Orchestra (billed as Les Brown and His Band of Renown)—in addition to Andy Kirk and His Twelve Clouds of Joy.

A MELLOW BIT OF RHYTHM
(1 9 3 7)

Mary Lou Williams

Mary Lou Williams

Mary Lou Williams

Mary Lou Williams

Mary Lou Williams

Mary Lou Williams

Mary Lou Williams

Mary Lou Williams

Mary Lou Williams

Mary Lou Williams

A MELLOW BIT OF RHYTHM (1937)

Mary Lou Williams

Mary Lou Williams

Primary Source.   MLWC: Autograph score in Williams's hand, on "Passantino Brands Dance Score #60" paper. The score is in oblong format with sixteen staves per page and consists of fifteen pages (eight predrawn measures per page). The paper provides a "Composition" (Title) line at the top left and a "Page" line at the top right. The "Composition" line reads "A Mellow Bit of Rythm" [*sic*] at the top of the first page; the pages are numbered on each "Page" line with a roman numeral I on the front page but arabic numerals 2–15 on subsequent pages. Williams provides no continuous measure count but starting at m. 9 (top of p. 2) she labels sections A–D, corresponding to sections of the present edition as follows: A = A1, B = A2, C = A3, and D = A4.

Instrumentation.   Alto Saxophone (doubling clarinet), Tenor Saxophones 1–2 (TSax 2 doubling clarinet), Baritone Saxophone (doubling ASax), Trumpets 1–3, Trombones 1–3, Bass, Guitar, Drums, Piano. The Trombone 3 part is written on the topmost staff (pre-labeled for "Violins A"), and the Baritone Saxophone part is written on the "Sax I" line.

Secondary Sources.   (1) BGP: Nearly complete set of parts on "King Brand No. 1" paper, all bearing #157 for band catalogue. Alto I, Tenor III, Tenor IV, Baritone; Trumpet I-II-III; Trombone I-II; Piano; Guitar; Bass; Drums; copyist unknown. Missing only Alto II.

(2) BGP: Autograph parts exist in this set for 3rd Alto (4th Tenor), Baritone, 2nd Trumpet, and Guitar on "Passantino Brand No. 1—12 Stave Medium" paper; each of these extra parts has the further distinguishing feature of a stamp bearing, in script, "Arranged and Composed by Mary Lou Williams." A fragment of what appears to be Page 2 of a Bass part exists on unidentified paper (though it is likely Passantino Brand No. 1—12 Stave Medium, given its similar configuration, Williams's handwriting, and the similar stamp that appears).

(3) BGP: Additional parts and fragments exist on "Parchment Brand #3—12 lines" paper: the first page of an Alto (Clarinet) part, and fragments of a Baritone part exist on two pages of unidentified paper, though this paper appears identical in size and layout to the Parchment Brand #3 paper described above.

(4) MLWC: Complete score compiled from an unknown set of parts by Steve Benson, c. 1991, on "Archives SP18S" paper; instrumentation is Alto 1–2, Tenor 1–2, Trumpets 1–3, Trombones 1–3, Guitar, Bass, Drums, Piano; see also corresponding letter and errata sheet by Benson, dated 8/5/91.

Two factors recommend the "Passantino Brands Dance Score #60" source over the set of parts on "King Brand No. 1" paper as the work's primary source for this volume. First, the score is in Mary Lou Williams's hand. Second, the score arrangement was written for and recorded in 1937 by Andy Kirk's band, of which Williams was a playing member, and for which she served as chief arranger. Conversely, the "King" parts comprise an arrangement Williams provided for Benny Goodman's band that he did not record. The arrangement for Goodman is in many ways the same, with slight modifications for differing instrumentation (five saxophones instead of four) and reed instrument doublers (in Kirk's band, the ASax 1 and TSax 2 double on clarinet in the arrangement, while in Goodman's band the ASax 2 and BSax parts contain the clarinet doubling), and small changes in rhythmic notation or pitch in a few passages.

It is also worth noting that the personnel of Andy Kirk's Clouds of Joy and the instrumentation listed in the primary source diverge in one respect: Williams writes for a third trombone that Kirk did not have. While this fact shows that Williams conceived her arrangement with slightly richer voicings in mind than Kirk could supply, it also may reveal her interest in making the arrangement more attractive to other bands that did carry three trombones.

Significant discrepancies between the primary source and the recording are discussed below, in a section labeled "Alternate Readings in Recording."

Critical Notes

Intro/1: Williams's score makes no reference to tempo. The tempo indicated in this edition is based on Kirk's 1937 recording, and was measured using a Qwik Time QT7 quartz metronome.

Intro/1.1, B: E♭ appears as in the primary source; note lies below range of the double bass, which ends on E, unless equipped with a C extension, uncommon among jazz bassists, especially at this time. E♭ is also called for at Intro/3 and A1/19, 21, and 23.

A1/1.1–2, Saxes: indication "(SLUR)." Slur markings replace this and all later "SLUR" indications where they occur in this arrangement.

A1/7.4, BSax: *marcato* marking.

A1/10.2, Tpts: b♭s in parentheses in source; notes seem wrong in all parts, as Tpts are contributing to unison gesture in horns. Both secondary sources show pitch c′ notated for Tpts.

A1/18.4, ASax 1: half note g′ and small, circled script "G" above staff; despite appearance of such clarity, G sounds wrong in context: Saxes are moving together in unison (octaves), completing phrase that ends with measure.

A1/24.5, ASax 1: f′ and d′; f′ has been scribbled out; script "F" above, and, in red ink, a check mark. The d′ (concert pitch f′) fits the musical line.

A1/25.1, Pn (LH): hard to read.

X1/1, Dr: *fake* 6.

X1/6.2–4, Tpt 1: c″–b♭′; mistakenly written at concert pitch.

X1/7.1, Tpt 1: "Unison."

A2/7.1 and 9.1, TSax 1: f″; here replaced by slash notation with chord symbol.

A2/19–25.1, TSax 1: TSax 1 playing in unison with TSax 2 and ASax 1 (and in octaves with BSax). It is more likely, however, that during the return to beginning of A2 section, Williams intended TSax 1 to resume the solo it began at start of this chorus (interrupted by Tpt 2 solo into bridge section of that chorus). An ossia staff provides solo chord changes and slash notation.

A2/19–24, Gtr, Pn, B: "Repeat 6 of B" (corresponding to A2/1–6).

A3/1–24, Gtr, Pn, B: "Fake 30," here replaced by chord changes and slash notation derived from Cl 2 and overall harmony.

A3/6.1–2, Cl 2: chord F6 on 6.1 and F7 on 6.2.

X2/2.2, Brass, Pn: end of dashed crescendo line.

X2/3.3, Gtr: "Cmi."

A4/3.4, Pn (LH): quarter rest missing.

A4/10.3, Gtr: chord symbol F♯dim; here enharmonically changed to be consistent with A4/12.3.

A4/15, beats 3–4: A♭m6 chord in Saxes and A♭6 chord in Trb 2, Gtr, Pn; secondary source shows same problem as primary. To correct this apparent mistake, pitches in Trb 2 and Pn were changed and additional chord symbol added to Gtr.

A4/19.8, Saxes: erroneously written as quarter note; secondary source confirms eighth note.

A4/20, Dr: "Swing 11."

A4/22.1, Tpt 2: e′.

A4/22.1, Trb 3: half note and no rests in this measure.

A4/23.3, Pn (LH): quarter note B has been inserted, as source shows only three beats in this staff.

A4/23.4, Pn (RH): a♭ and e′; here replaced by a and e♭′ in this chord voicing to agree with intended B7 chord in Gtr (a is 7th, e♭′ is 3rd, spelled enharmonically).

A4/24.1, Pn (RH): illegible; harmony provided here follows chord symbol E7 above stave.

A4/28–32: measures not written out, as (starting A4/25) Williams returns to head melody (the eight-bar *a* section). On the source's last score page Williams writes the first three measures of this reprise (compare A4/25–27 with A1/1–3, allowing for the slight rhythmic modification in A4/25), and then writes in the margin, "To 2nd ending for end FINE," meaning that the piece is to conclude with the second ending heard in the head chorus, A1/9–10. But if followed precisely, her directive to jump to this second ending would create a five-bar final phrase. Moreover, to play the entire second ending, including the last note of A1/10 with its B♭7 chord, the dominant in the key of E♭, would lead back into A1/11 and the music that follows. Andy Kirk's recording of this arrangement shows that neither was intended. Therefore the edition presents the entire eight-measure phrase and ends without the last chord. However, because A4/26 does not show the brass figure, it is omitted too at A4/28 and the piano line continued as in A4/25–27. The last note in the Pn (LH) and Bass is also moved an eighth note ahead to correspond with the other instruments. Finally, however, the recording reveals one more discrepancy. When A1/9–10 is first heard, the reeds and brass play the melodic figure in unison (octaves) as notated. However, at the end of the recording, the reeds and brass play the entire figure in a harmonized soli, with the lead melodic line an octave higher than in the original line. In the edition I also provide my own transcription of the final two measures of the Andy Kirk recording as an alternative ending. It bears resemblance to the Goodman arrangement (see secondary sources (1)–(3)) as well as the score compiled by Steve Benson (secondary source (4)) but also contains several differences.

Alternate Readings in Recording

A1/6, Brass: three-eighth-note unison figure played exactly as in A1/2 and A1/4. This is reflected in both secondary sources as well, seeming to indicate a change favored by Williams after she had first completed the arrangement.

A3/6–24: cut to reduce length; specifically, during second time through passage beginning at A3/1 (Cl solo), brass omit three-eighth-note gesture at end of A3/6, and ensemble jumps to X2/1. The cut reduces Cl solo from thirty measures to fourteen.

MESSA STOMP (1938)

For Andy Kirk. Edited from 1942 Manuscript

Composer. Mary Lou Williams

Primary Source. Autograph score in Williams's hand in spiral-bound manuscript book. Mary Lou Williams Collection, Institute of Jazz Studies, Rutgers University, Newark, NJ

Date of Composition. Uncertain; probably 1938

Recording. Decca 2204, matrix 64615-A, reissued as Classics Records, Classics 598 (compact disc, 1991)

Date and Location of Recording. 9 September 1938, New York City

Band. Andy Kirk and His Twelve Clouds of Joy

Personnel. Harry Lawson, Clarence Trice, Earl Thompson, trumpets; Ted Donnelly, Henry Wells, trombones; John Harrington, clarinet/alto saxophone; Earl Miller, alto saxophone; Dick Wilson, tenor saxophone; John Williams, baritone saxophone; Mary Lou Williams, piano; Ted Brinson, guitar; Booker Collins, bass; Ben Thigpen, drums

Form. Key B♭: Intro$_{(4)}$ A1$_{(Cl, 12)}$ A2$_{(Cl, 12)}$ Key Gm: X$_{(4)}$ B1$_{(8)}$ B2$_{(Tpt, 8)}$ Key B♭: A3$_{(Pn, 12)}$ A4$_{(Pn, 12)}$ C1$_{(12)}$ C2$_{(12)}$ A5$_{(Gtr, 13)}$ A6$_{(12)}$ A7$_{(12)}$ A8$_{(12)}$ Tag$_{(Cl, 4)}$

The 1938 date of composition is based on the recording date of 9 September 1938, even as the written sources themselves, which I have named the "Pittsburgh Notebooks," are believed to date from shortly after Mary Lou Williams left Andy Kirk and His Clouds of Joy in 1942. The address written inside the front cover of the primary source, "510 Winfield Street," was the residence of her Aunt Mamie, to which she repaired for a short time at this unhappy moment. Leaving the band on less than friendly terms, she did not take her arrangements with her when she left, but she did write down a number of them in two notebooks. In the one used here as the primary source for *Messa Stomp*, she also included versions of *Rhythm Crazy*, *After You've Gone*, *Ghost of Love*, and a portion of *I've Found a New Love Now*. In the other book (missing the front cover and index page) she wrote arrangements of *Mary's Idea*, *Toadie Toddle*, *Ghost of Love*, *What's Your Story, Morning Glory?*, and part of an untitled work, as well as a version of *Messa Stomp* that is used as the secondary source for this composition. All material contained in this edition derives from the primary source except Williams's piano solo, which I have transcribed from the recording. After Williams left the Kirk band, her arrangements lost their place as a central part of the Clouds' repertory.

MESSA STOMP

(1 9 3 8)

Mary Lou Williams

MESSA STOMP (1938)

Mary Lou Williams

Mary Lou Williams

Mary Lou Williams

Mary Lou Williams

Mary Lou Williams

Mary Lou Williams

Mary Lou Williams

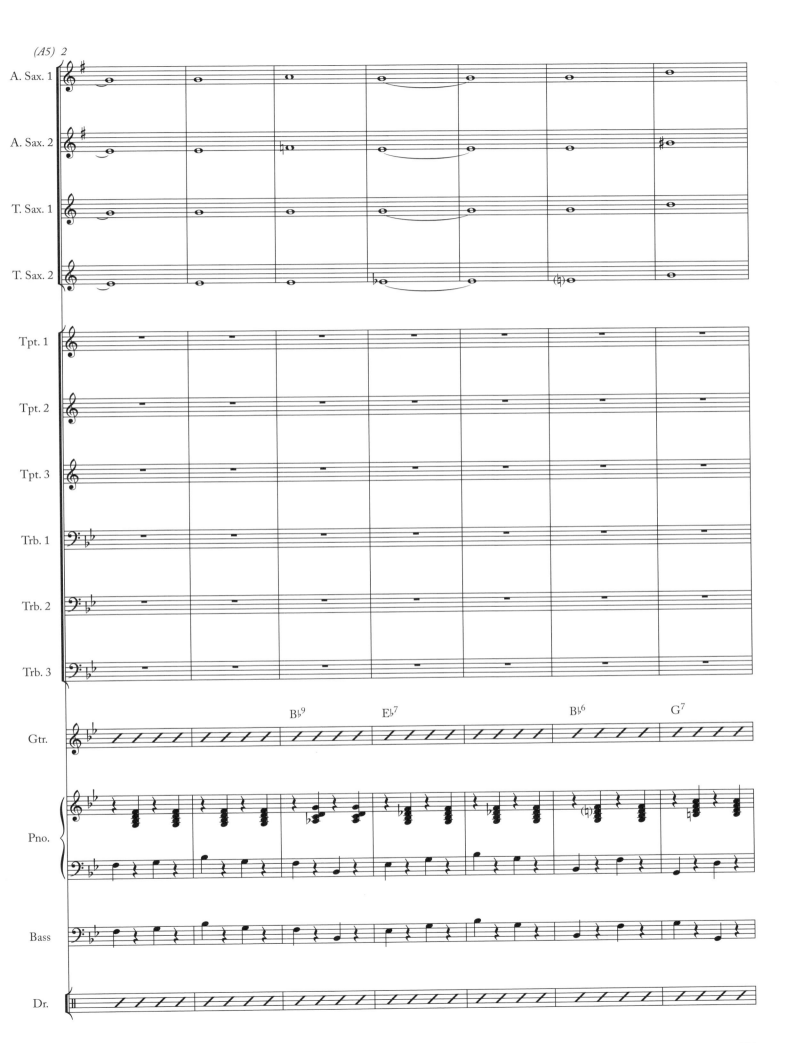

MESSA STOMP (1938)

Mary Lou Williams

MESSA STOMP (1938)

Mary Lou Williams

Mary Lou Williams

138   Mary Lou Williams

Mary Lou Williams

Primary Source.   MLWC: Spiral-bound manuscript score book published under the name "La Lumia's Score Book" in Chicago. The book has a green cover with a large treble clef symbol and the words "Mary Lou William's [*sic*] Score Book" professionally printed on it. The words "Book II" are written in pencil on the front cover, as are miscellaneous handwritten scribbles that include "89¢," "44¢," and "68¢." Inside the front cover, an "Index" page lists six arrangements, of which *Messa Stomp* is the first. The phrase "Arranged and Composed by Mary Lou Williams" is stamped in four places on this page, and an address (510 Winfield Street) and an enigmatic string of characters (H19 4949) are handwritten there too. The score is in portrait format with seventeen staves per page and consists of thirty-five pages (alternating four and five predrawn measures per page). The paper provides preformatted staff systems for three violins, four saxophones, three trumpets, three trombones (1st and 3rd on one staff, 2nd on another), guitar, bass (or tuba), drums (or bells), and piano (or harp). Williams's arrangement uses the staves mostly as marked except that she writes the Trombone 3 part on one violin staff and the solo clarinet part (doubled by Alto Saxophone 2) on another. The title appears at the top of the first score page. Williams provides no measure or page count, but she labels sections in a way corresponding to the present edition as follows: A = A1, B = A2, C = X, D = B1/B2, E = A3, F = A4, G = C1/C2, H = A5, I = A6, J = A7, K = A8.

Instrumentation.   Alto Saxophone 1, Alto Saxophone 2/Clarinet, Tenor Saxophones 1–2, Trumpets 1–3, Trombones 1–3, Guitar, Piano, Bass, Drums.

Secondary Source.   MLWC: Autograph score in Williams's hand in spiral-bound manuscript book published under the name "La Lumia's Score Book" in Chicago. This book's formatting is identical to the primary source except that it lacks a cover.

These two notebooks, apparently written from memory and after the fact, are the earliest surviving sources of Williams's output during the twelve years she spent with Andy Kirk's band. It is not known why she chose to write down the arrangement to *Messa Stomp* twice, especially since a comparison of the two reveals both striking similarities and a few stark differences. One notable difference between the two versions of the written-out arrangement is length: one source is twelve measures longer than the other. There are also incongruities between the two written versions and the Clouds of Joy recording of the arrangement. In both versions of the arrangement Williams indicates a reed section of two altos and two tenors (with reed doubling indicated in the parts). Yet the personnel reported in every discography for the recording (and reproduced above) points to a saxophone distribution of two altos, one tenor, and one baritone. In fact, the same discrepancy between source material and discographical information exists for Williams's second arrangement of *Mary's Idea*, a counterpart of *Messa Stomp*. And a full set of parts exists for the 1938 *Mary's Idea* that also calls for two alto and two tenor saxophones, with the second alto doubling on baritone saxophone. These parts lend support to the similar instrumentation Williams provides in *Messa Stomp*, and in the absence of aural evidence on the recording to the contrary, I remain true to the AATT distribution that appears in both versions in the notebooks.

The edition of the 1938 *Messa Stomp* in this volume gives preference to the source that contains extra material. Being aware of the time limitations of recordings from this era, I tend to assume that the "extra" material would have been played in most settings and was cut only for the recording. In this case, the secondary source is the more consistent with the recorded version of the arrangement.

Significant discrepancies between the sources and the recording are given special treatment below, in a section labeled "Alternate Readings in Secondary Source and Recording," while more minor discrepancies are not noted, as a rule.

Intro/1: Williams's score makes no reference to tempo. The tempo indicated in this edition is based on Kirk's 1938 recording, and was measured using a Qwik Time QT7 quartz metronome.

A1/1, Dr: "Swing 8."

A1/2.1–2, Tpts, Trb: indication "SLUR." Slur markings replace this and all later "SLUR" indications where they occur in this arrangement.

A1/10.3, Gtr: chord symbol F7+.

A1/11–12, Cl: "out - - - - ."

A2/10.1, Pn (LH), B: edition presents pitch as in primary source; E♭ may be regarded as accented passing tone between previous D (which functions as root of the D6 chord in question) and approaching F.

B1/7.2–8, Trbs: "Closed (C), Open (O)" and subsequent alternation of "C" and "O"; here replaced by more customary + and o symbols.

B1/8, Pn (RH): blank measure.

B2/8.1, Pn (LH): quarter note; here shortened due to written-out solo (see following notes).

B2/8.2, ASax 1: "Piano."

B2/8.2–A4/12, Pn: primary source notates LH same as Bass (except as mentioned in subsequent critical notes) and provides chord symbols; here replaced by Williams's piano solo, transcribed from the 9 September 1938 recording (see "Recording," above).

A3/12, fourth beat–A4/1, first beat, Pn: chord notated in two tied quarter notes, reading from bottom to top B♭+f (LH), f+b♭+d′+g′ (RH).

A4/2, fourth beat–3, first beat, Pn: same chord as two measures before (see note above).

A4/11.1, Pn: quarter-note chord, LH/RH same as described above for A3/12.

A4/11, second beat, Pn: "break," as no instrument is indicated to play before upbeat to C1.

A4/12, second half of third beat, Pn: chord notated as dotted quarter note, reading from bottom to top F+f (LH), a+c′+e♭′+f′ (RH).

C2/1–10, Gtr, Pn, B: "Fake 10" followed by blank measures; as this passage covers same harmonic and melodic ground as C1/1–10 this edition replicates these measures here.

C2/8.2, Trb 3: "muted."

C2/11, third and fourth beats, Gtr: chord symbols C♯dim-Cm7; as chord voicings of Pn (RH) show a Cm7-C♯dim progression (doubled by Tpts) the Gtr chords were changed accordingly. Saxes (in unison), Trbs, Pn (LH), and B, however, outline notes that imply Cm7-F7. In the secondary source all chord symbols and voicings corroborate Cm7-F7.

C2/12.1, Dr: blank measure.

A5/13, Gtr: blank measure.

A5/13.3, Dr: "go to town."

A5/13.4, Tpt 1: "swingy"; here applied to entire score.

A6/1.4, Tpts: "smear"; here realized with glissando marking and applied to all wind instruments.

A6/11.4–12.5, Saxes, Trbs: figure placed in parenthesis and annotation "out." The primary source shows a layer of corrections in dark ink, possibly made after the first notation, which shows less dark ink. As the marking "out" was written with lighter ink, and as corrections of this fill were made with the darker ink, this edition provides the notes of the fill. Williams wrote a similar saxophone fill in the secondary sources to complement the Trbs. In the Clouds of Joy recording only the Trbs play the fill (see "Alternate Readings" at the end of this commentary).

A6/12.1, Pn: chord symbol E♭6.

A7/8.3, Pn: chord symbol B♭dim.

A8/2.1 and 4.2, Pn: chord symbol A6.

Alternate Readings in Secondary Source and Recording

Intro/1–4: not found in recording, which begins with the anacrusis chord to measure 5, played by the brass and rhythm section.

B2/1–7.2, Tpt 3: plunger solo given to Tpt 2 in secondary source.

C1/10–12: secondary source reads as shown in Example 1 below (Gtr, Pn, B, Dr as in primary source). The recording more closely resembles the alternate version.

C2/12–A5/10: secondary source eliminates Gtr solo and instead provides a two-measure unison chromatic Sax gesture (see Example 2 below). Recording is consistent with secondary source.

A6/8–11.3, TSaxes: parts are swapped in secondary source.

A6/11–12.5, Saxes, Trbs: see below for the alternate realizations of this passage in the secondary source (Example 3) and the recording (Example 4).

A8/1–5.1, TSaxes: parts are swapped in secondary source, placing higher line in TSax 1 and lower line in TSax 2.

A8/9–end: ending in secondary source differs considerably: it is shorter by two bars, eliminates the reprise of the Cl solo, and alters the voicings of several lines and chords.

Example 1.

Example 2.

Example 3.

Example 4.

MARY'S IDEA (1938)

For Andy Kirk. Edited from 1942 Manuscript

Composer.   Mary Lou Williams

Primary Source.   Autograph score in Williams's hand in spiral-bound manuscript book. Mary Lou Williams Collection, Institute of Jazz Studies, Rutgers University, Newark, NJ

Date of Composition.   Uncertain; probably 1938

Recording.   Decca 2326, matrix 64783-A, reissued as Classics Records, Classics 598 (compact disc, 1991)

Date and Location of Recording.   6 December 1938, New York City

Band.   Andy Kirk and His Twelve Clouds of Joy

Personnel.   Harry Lawson, Clarence Trice, Earl Thompson, trumpets; Ted Donnelly, Henry Wells, trombones; John Harrington, Earl Miller, alto saxophones; John Williams, baritone saxophone; Dick Wilson, tenor saxophone; Mary Lou Williams, piano; Ted Brinson, guitar; Booker Collins, bass; Ben Thigpen, drums

Form.   Key E♭: Intro$_{(4)}$ A1$_{(8+8+8+8=32)}$ A2$_{(\text{Tpt}, 8+8+8+8=32)}$ X1$_{(\text{Cl}, 8+8=16)}$ A3$_{(\text{TSax, Trb,}}$ $_{8+8+8+8=32)}$ X2$_{(4)}$ A4$_{(8+8+8+8=32)}$ Tag$_{(6)}$

The 1938 date of composition is based on the recording date of 6 December 1938. As a reworking of her 1930 composition of the same name, the work demonstrates the evolution of Williams's composition and arranging style from 1930 to 1938. The essay introducing this volume compares the two versions. Like the source for *Messa Stomp*, the primary source for *Mary's Idea* dates from a time shortly after Williams left Andy Kirk and His Twelve Clouds of Joy in 1942, when Williams lived temporarily in Pittsburgh. The arrangement was written in one of the two spiral-bound notebooks Williams used there. Presumably, not having her arrangements from the Kirk band with her (see commentary for *Messa Stomp*) she wrote the one for *Mary's Idea* from memory. The set of parts serving as a secondary source for this edition is useful, for the many performance markings attest to frequent use. However, the set is woefully incomplete.

MARY'S IDEA

(1 9 3 8)

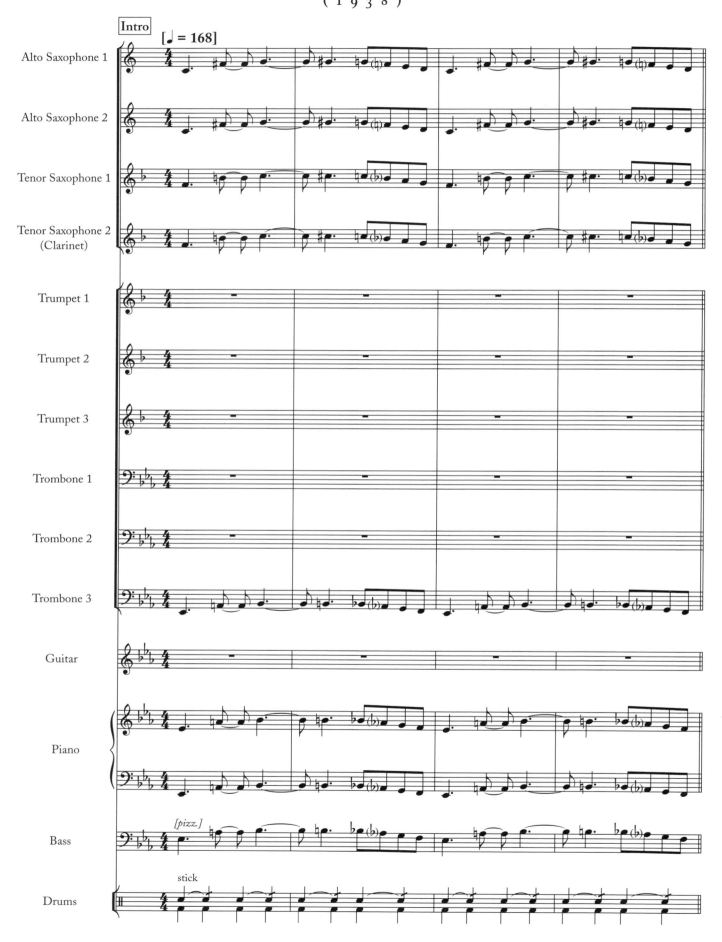

148   Mary Lou Williams

Mary's Idea (1938)

Mary Lou Williams

MARY'S IDEA (1938)

Mary Lou Williams

Mary Lou Williams

Mary Lou Williams

Mary Lou Williams

MARY'S IDEA (1938)

Mary Lou Williams

Mary Lou Williams

Mary Lou Williams

Mary Lou Williams

MARY'S IDEA (1938)

Mary Lou Williams

MARY'S IDEA (1938)

Mary Lou Williams

Mary Lou Williams

Primary Source.   MLWC: Spiral-bound manuscript score book published under the name "La Lumia's Score Book" in Chicago. The score is in portrait format with seventeen staves per page and consists of twenty-nine pages (alternating four and five predrawn measures per page), although the first page has torn away from the spiral binding and is ripped in several places. The paper provides preformatted staff systems for three violins, four saxophones, three trumpets, three trombones (1st and 3rd on one staff, 2nd on another), guitar, bass (or tuba), drums (or bells), and piano (or harp). Williams's arrangement uses the staves as marked except that she writes the Trombone 3 part on one violin staff. The title can be made out (despite the torn paper) at the top of the first page. Williams provides no measure or page count, but she labels sections in a way corresponding to the present edition as follows: A = A1, B = A2, C = X1, D = A3/X2, E = A4.

Instrumentation.   Alto 1–2, Tenor 1, Tenor 2 (with doubling on clarinet), Trumpets 1–3, Trombones 1–3, Guitar, Piano, Bass, Drums.

Secondary Source.   MLWC: Incomplete set of parts in Williams's hand on "Premier Brand No. 101—12 Lines" paper. Instrumentation includes: Alto 1, Alto 2 (with doubling on Baritone), Tenor 1 (also labeled "Dick"), Tenor 2 (with doubling on clarinet), Trumpet 3, and Trombone (part corresponds with Trombone 1 of the score in primary source, above).

Critical Notes

Intro/1: Williams's score makes no reference to tempo. The tempo indicated in this edition is based on Kirk's 1938 recording, and was measured using a Qwik Time QT7 quartz metronome.

A1/5–6, Trb 3: missing measures, see comment for A1/9–10.

A1/9–10, Trb 3: missing measures. Williams marked a repeat for A1/1–8 with repeat signs and only wrote out two measures for a varied second ending. She then, however, decided also to vary A1/5–6 in the repeat. Rather than inserting these two measures in their entirety, Williams wrote the different brass section in condensed format in the top two violin staves at A1/5–6, along with a reference indicating where these measures are to be inserted. However, as it seems that Williams added a Trb 3 line later, she forgot to write out A1/5–6 and 9–10. As Trb 3 follows ASax 1 in all other tutti passages, these missing measures were derived here from the ASax 1 line.

A1/11.6, TSax 2: a′ likely an error; all other Saxes sound in unison.

A1/13.5, TSax 2: e″ likely an error.

A1/19.1, Gtr: chord symbol F.

A1/21–24, Saxes: "Copy 4 of A" (here A1/1–4).

A1/21–25, Brass and rhythm sections: "Copy 5 of A" (here A1/1–5).

A1/25.4, TSax 2: accent.

A1/26.1, Trb 2: note missing; see comment for Trb 3 in next critical note.

A1/26.1–27.1, Trb 3: appears in primary source in Trb 2 staff. That the part was not meant for Trb 2 is indicated by first note b♭, which does not align with last note of Trb 2 from A1/25. This b♭ is reproduced here an octave lower, as preceding Trb 3 part is an octave lower.

A1/27, Tpt 3: "Mute" written above blank measure, but solo by Tpt 3 on Kirk's recording is unmuted.

A1/28, Tpt 3: opening gesture of improvised solo notated in eighth notes: c″–d″–f″–g″–f″–g″–a″; here replaced by slash notation.

A2/1–7.1, Trb 3: appears in primary source on Trb 2 staff; part assigned here to Trb 3, which consistently joins with Saxes in tutti passages.

A2/2.1, Trb 3: d♭′, which does not fit B♭9 harmony (the editorial c′ is the 9th).

A2/6.3–4, ASaxes, Trb 3: "slur" and slur markings. ASax 1 slur removed as tone repetitions are being played. "Slur" instruction removed and replaced by slur marking in all similar situations in this arrangement.

A2/9.1, TSaxes: TSax 1 has e♭ and TSax 2 has g.

A2/9.1, Tpt 3: chord symbol E♭6.

A2/10.1–2, Trbs, Tpts 1–2: glissando replaces the following markings: Tpt 1 has slur only, Tpt 2 has nothing, Trb 1 has slur and "smear," Trbs 2–3 have only annotation "smear."

A2/11–end, Pn (RH): blank measures; replaced here with chord symbols and slash notation (matching Gtr), directing pianist to continue same style of accompaniment.

A2/12.1–2, Tpt 1, Trb 3: "slur" indicated; not applied here as tone repetitions are being played.

A2/12.4, Trb 3: accent.

A2/15.4, Pn (LH), B: Pn slash on this beat, B quarter rest. There being no reason to interrupt the walking bass line that precedes it, the pitch d is provided as a note in the B♭7 harmony that also continues the descending stepwise motion between e♭ and c.

A2/19–23, Saxes: "Copy 5 of B" (here A2/1–5).

A2/19–23, Trb 3: "Copy 5 of A," actually written in the system of Trb 1; reference to "A" is an error, "B" is correct (here A2/1–5).

A2/24–25.1, Trb 3: blank measure; notation copied here from A2/6–7.1, with rhythm adjusted to the Saxes.

A2/25.1, Tpt 3: c″; here replaced by slash notation.

A2/26.6, ASax 1: marcato.

X1/9.3–4, Trb 2: eighth notes, leaving too few beats in measure.

X1/12.2, Tpt 3: f♯′ (concert e′), likely a mistake as it does not fit the prevailing F9 harmony.

X1/15–16, Dr: difficult to read.

A3/1–10, TSax 1: "Tenor Solo" and blank measures; here chord symbols and slash notation added.

A3/1.3–4, Tpt 1: o and + followed by "etc." The order of the symbols, seemingly an error, is reversed here.

A3/1–10, Tpts 2–3, Trbs 1–2: no mute symbols.

A3/1–9, Pn (LH): blank measures; here replaced by duplication of Bass line.

A3/11–18, Trb 3: "3rd Trb Solo 8" and blank measures, with chord symbols in A3/15–16; here slash notation and additional chord symbols added.

A3/19–24, Saxes, Brass, and rhythm section: "Repeat 6 of D" (here A3/1–6).

A3/25–end, Pn (LH): blank measures; here replaced by duplication of Bass line.

A3/25–26.1, TSax 1: rest.

A3/25–26.1, Tpt 3: blank.

A3/26–X2/4, ASax 2: "Colla Sax I."

A3/26–X2/4, TSax 1: "Unison."

A3/26–X2/4, TSax 2: squiggly line indicating unison with other Saxes.

A4/1–6.1, ASax 2: "Colla" (interpreted as unison with ASax 1).

A4/1–4, TSax 1: "Colla" (interpreted as unison with ASax 1).

A4/5.1, TSaxes: f′; as previous measure ends with b♭′, pitch is corrected.

A4/11.2, 11.4, 12.2, 13.2, Pn, B: slash notation.

A4/14.4, ASaxes: f′; here corrected to g′ as an upbeat to extended unison passage for all Saxes.

A4/15, B: illegible note.

A4/15–Tag/2, ASax 2, TSax 1: "Colla" (interpreted as unison with ASax 1).

A4/15–Tag/2, TSax 2: squiggly line (interpreted as unison with ASax 1).

A4/15–17, Tpts, Trbs: + and o marking provided only for Tpt 1; here applied to all.

A4/16.1–17.4, Tpt 1: markings start with + and end with + on 17.4; here changed to alternate continuously.

A4/18.1, Tpt 1: quarter note; here replaced by eighth note for consistency.

A4/23.3, B: A♭; replaced by A♮ for consistency with Adim harmony.

A4/23.4–25.1, Gtr: b♭′.

Tag/3–6, Dr: snare uses "x" noteheads.

Tag/4.4–5.1, Gtr: f♯′–f♮′.

Tag/5.2–3, TSax 1: f′–a′; likely errors as all other Saxes play in octaves.

Tag/6.1–3, Gtr: b♭′–c″; second chord symbol reads only E♭.

SCORPIO (1946)

For Duke Ellington. Edited from Manuscript

Composer. Mary Lou Williams

Primary Source. Autograph score in Williams's hand. Duke Ellington Collection, Smithsonian National Museum of American History Archives Center, Washington, D.C.

Date of Composition. Uncertain; probably 1946

Recording. No studio recording of this composition exists from Williams's lifetime. A recording was made in 2005 by the Dutch Jazz Orchestra, Challenge Records CR73251 (compact disc).

Form. Key B♭m: Intro$_{(4+4=8)}$ A$_{(18)}$ B$_{(14)}$ Key G♭: C$_{(20)}$ Key B♭: D$_{(10)}$

S*corpio* departs from Williams's earlier big band compositional style, testifying that modernist art music was influencing her by the second half of the 1940s. This piece was originally part of the twelve-movement *Zodiac Suite* that she composed and performed with a piano trio, recording the work in June 1945. During the summer and fall, Williams revised and performed the entire suite with a chamber orchestra fronted by a jazz combo. That version was part of a concert at New York City's Town Hall on New Year's Eve, 1945. In the following year, she expanded the instrumentation again, rescoring this movement for the Duke Ellington Orchestra. Judging from the relatively clean condition of the set of parts in the Ellington Collection, it is doubtful that the orchestra performed this work frequently, if at all. In this arrangement, Williams explores an unusual variety of timbres and colors in the ensemble, demonstrating a much freer approach to dissonance—both melodic and harmonic—than in her earlier work. Additionally, while the composition is grounded in two bass ostinati, the overall form is through-composed. All these traits indicate that the modernist art music Williams was studying at the time was having an impact on her approach to composition.

SCORPIO

(1 9 4 6)

Mary Lou Williams

182   Mary Lou Williams

184

Mary Lou Williams

Mary Lou Williams

Scorpio (1946)

Mary Lou Williams

Primary Source.   DEC: Autograph score on "King Brand No. 35" paper. The score is in oblong format with nineteen staves per page and consists of nine pages (eight pre-drawn measures per page). The paper provides preformatted staff systems for up to six saxophones, four trumpets, four trombones, guitar, piano, bass, and drums; Williams uses only the first five saxophone staves and on each page adjusts the formatting for trumpets and trombones by writing "5" (intended for Trumpet 5) over "1" (intended for Trombone 1), and likewise writes "1," "2," and "3" over "2," "3," and "4" at the left margin of each remaining trombone staff (see Instrumentation, below). The title is written at the top center of each page with a page number adjacent. Williams writes "Hamilton" adjacent to the Tenor Saxophone 1 label on p. 1, a reference to Ellington tenor saxophonist Jimmy Hamilton. Likewise, Williams writes "Ray" adjacent to the Trumpet 5 label on p. 1, a reference to Ellington trumpeter/violinist Ray Nance. Williams provides no continuous measure count, but she labels sections, starting at m. 8 (top of p. 2), in a way corresponding to the present edition as follows: A = A, B = B, C = C (located two measures earlier), and D = D.

Instrumentation.   Alto Saxophones 1–2, Tenor Saxophone 1 (with doubling on clarinet), Tenor Saxophone 2, Baritone Saxophone (with doubling on clarinet), Trumpets 1–5, Trombones 1–3, Guitar, Piano, Bass, Drums.

Secondary Sources.   (1) DEC: Incomplete set of parts in unknown copyist's hand, labeled #251 for band catalogue, on "Duke Ellington signature/Passantino No. 1—12 Stave Medium" paper. Parts include "Pro" (Russell Procope, Alto 1), "Rab" (Johnny Hodges, Alto 2), "Jimmy" (Jimmy Hamilton, Tenor 1, with clarinet doubling), "Sears" (Al Sears, Tenor 2), "Carney" (Harry Carney, Baritone, with clarinet doubling), "Cat" (Cat Anderson, Trumpet 1), "Scad" (Shelton Hemphill, Trumpet 2), "Williams" (Francis Williams, Trumpet 3), "Taft" (Taft Jordan, Trumpet 4), "Ray" (Ray Nance, Trumpet 5), "Jones" (Claude Jones, Trombone 2), "Wilbur" (Wilbur De Paris, Trombone 3), Guitar, Bass. Part for Trombone 1 is missing.

(2) MLWC: Complete score transcribed into and printed from computer music notation software, transcriber unknown. Original source of transcription unknown, but possibly derives from the primary source or the set of parts listed above. Subtitled "Arranged for Duke Ellington (1946)." Bound with black plastic binding. Instrumentation: Alto Saxophones 1–2, Tenor Saxophone 1 (with doubling on clarinet), Tenor Saxophone 2, Baritone Saxophone (with doubling on clarinet), Trumpets 1–5, Trombones 1–3, Guitar, Piano, Bass, Drums.

(3) MLWC: Complete set of parts in Williams's hand on "King Brand No. 1" paper for Andy Kirk and His Clouds of Joy. Parts include Conductor's score reduction (labeled "Andy"), 1st Alto (Alto Saxophone 1), 3rd Alto (Alto Saxophone 2, with doubling on clarinet), Tenor (Tenor Saxophone 1, with doubling on clarinet), II Tenor (Tenor Saxophone 2), Baritone Saxophone, Trumpets 1–4, Trombones 1–3, Guitar, Piano, Bass, Drums.

(4) DEC: Complete score in unknown hand on "King Brand No. M-2—10-Stave" paper. Instrumentation for jazz combo: Alto Saxophone, Tenor Saxophone (doubling on clarinet), Baritone Saxophone (doubling on Clarinet), Trumpets 1–2, Trombone, Bass, Piano.

(5) DEC: Complete score in unknown hand on "Passantino Brand Number 1—12-Stave Medium" paper. Instrumentation for jazz combo: Trumpets (two trumpets written *divisi* on single staff), Alto Saxophone (doubling on clarinet), Tenor Saxophone (doubling on clarinet), Trombone, Bass.

The complete score in Williams's hand takes preference over either set of parts as the primary source. Items indicated in the score but not in the part may generally be attributed to copyist error. The parts listed as secondary source (1) are based on those listed as secondary source (3), as shown by errors in the latter that are similarly found in the former (e.g., articulations found in the score and inadvertently omitted from certain parts in one set are similarly omitted in the other set of parts).

Critical Notes

Intro/1.4, Tpts, Trbs 1–2: accent on second note of tied pair.

Intro/3.3, Dr: *f.*

Intro/3.5–4.1, Dr: "soft"; here replaced by *mp.*

Intro/4, Dr: recent performances of this composition interpret the drum notation to be played by timpani mallets on the toms.

B/1, ASaxes, TSaxes, Brass: inconsistent application of glissando markings (with annotation "lip," meaning a lip slur); here applied consistently in Saxes to first two notes (B/1.2–3) and in brass to first three notes (B/1.2–4).

B/1, B: *ff.*

B/1.4–5, Tpts 1–2: decrescendo marking; not in secondary source (1); here removed as overall effect suggests sudden change in dynamic at B/2, rather than gradual one.

B/3.1, B: *f.*

B/4.1–2, Pn (LH): G♭ half note; replaced by quarter notes G♭ and A♭$_1$ to double bass line.

B/11–14, Dr: tremolo marking for snare missing.

C/6.1, B: G♭ appears in source, likely an error; replaced with quarter rest for consistency with ensemble.

C/12–16, Pn (LH): "col Bass."

C/13, Tpt 5: " to violin." Tpt 5 part was written with Ellington trumpeter Ray Nance in mind (see description of primary source above), who also played violin. Since such a doubling is rare, the improvised violin solo might be taken over by trumpet.

C/15, ASax 1: one-measure *decrescendo.*

C/15–16, Trbs: *decrescendo* in C/15 followed by *diminuendo* marking in C/16; here replaced by two-measure *decrescendo.*

D/1.1, Dr: "soft"; here replaced by *mp.*

D/3–10, Vn: written block chord spellings meant to indicate "correct" notes with which to improvise. Here replaced by the modern practice of slash notation and chord symbols.

D/3–10.2, Pn (RH): written block chord spellings; here replaced by chord symbols and slash notation.

D/8, Pn (LH): empty measure.

D/10.2, Dr: half note and "cym." Here interpreted as cymbal roll.

LONELY MOMENTS (1947)

For Duke Ellington. Edited from Manuscript

Composer. Mary Lou Williams

Primary Source. Autograph score in Williams's hand. Duke Ellington Collection, Smithsonian National Museum of American History Archives Center, Washington, D.C.

Date of Composition. Uncertain; probably 1947

Recording. No studio recording of this composition exists from Williams's lifetime. A recording was made in 2005 by the Dutch Jazz Orchestra, Challenge Records CR73251 (compact disc). See Table 1 for recordings of other arrangements.

Form. Key Fm: Intro$_{(6)}$ A1$_{(8+8+8+8=32)}$ X$_{(4)}$ Key B♭m: A2$_{(Tpt, 8+8+8+8=32)}$ Key Fm: B$_{(Tpt, 24)}$ C$_{(Fugue, 6+6+6=18)}$ D$_{(8+6+8=22)}$

*L*onely *Moments* reflects Williams's interest in applying a combo style of modern jazz to a big band, and also her study of fugal technique, borrowed from Western music of the 1600s and 1700s. As the arrangement builds momentum toward its final, climactic statement, she introduces a near-textbook example of a fugal exposition in which trumpets, then saxophones, then trombones each present the same unison melody (a "subject"), continuing with an independent melody to create a web of counterpoint. Around the time of this arrangement for Ellington, Williams arranged *Lonely Moments* for the Benny Goodman Orchestra, and also for the Milton Orent-Frank Roth Orchestra (with instrumentation of Alto Saxophone, Tenor Saxophones 1–2, Baritone Saxophone, Trumpets 1–3, Piano, Bass, Drums). Neither arrangement survives, but both were recorded, as summarized in Table 1.[1] The fugal passage in the arrangement for Goodman is the same one found in the Ellington arrangement that appears here, but the corresponding passage Williams wrote for the Orent-Roth arrangement is completely different.

---

1. For a more thorough discussion of the various arrangements of *Lonely Moments* Williams prepared during this time period, please see my article *"Lonely Moments?* The Anatomy of Mary Lou Williams' Oft-Recorded Tune."

Table 1.   Mary Lou Williams's arrangements of *Lonely Moments*

Date	Band	Instrumentation	Recording Information (original/reissue)
1/13/47	Goodman orchestra	cl/aattb/4tpt/3trb/pgbd	First Heard FH23 (LP), Laserlight 15762 (CD)
1/22/47	Goodman orchestra	cl/aattb/4tpt/3trb/pgbd	Capitol Cap 374 (78), Cap T409 (LP), Capitol Jazz 7243-8-32086-2-3 (CD)
c. 1947 (date unknown)	Orent-Roth orchestra	attb/3tpt/pbd	Disc 6067 (78), Folkways FA-2966 (LP), Classics 1050 (CD)

LONELY MOMENTS
(1 9 4 7)

Mary Lou Williams

Mary Lou Williams

Lonely Moments (1947)

Mary Lou Williams

Mary Lou Williams

Mary Lou Williams

Lonely Moments (1947)

Mary Lou Williams

Mary Lou Williams

Mary Lou Williams

Mary Lou Williams

Mary Lou Williams

LONELY MOMENTS (1947)

216   Mary Lou Williams

LONELY MOMENTS (1947)

217

Primary Source.　DEC: Autograph score on "King Brand No. 35" paper. The score is in landscape format with nineteen staves per page and consists of fourteen pages (eight predrawn measures per page). The paper provides preformatted staff systems for Saxophones 1–5, Trumpets 1–4, Trombones 1–4, Guitar, Piano, Bass, and Drums. Williams's arrangement uses the staves as marked, except that the staff preformatted as Trombone 1 is used by Trumpet 5, and the three trombones used in the arrangement are shifted down one staff accordingly. The fourteen score pages are folded in half (book-style) so that the back of the last score page serves as a kind of title page. On this blank page (verso of score page 14) appears the title, "Lonely Moments," along with a name, Barbara Hillsman, and, elsewhere, the number "SC4-2021." The title appears at the top of the first page; page numbers and either the title or its abbreviation, "L.M.," are written at the top of subsequent pages. Williams provides no continuous measure count, but she labels sections, starting at m. 7, in a way corresponding to the present edition as follows: A = A1, B = A1/17, C = A2, D = A2/17, E = B, F = C, G = C/7, H = C/13, and I = D.

Instrumentation.　Alto Saxophone 1–2, Tenor Saxophone 1–2, Baritone Saxophone, Trumpet 1–5, Trombone 1–3, Guitar, Piano, Bass, Drums.

Secondary Sources.　(1) DEC: Incomplete set of parts in unknown copyist's hand, labeled #237 for band catalogue. All except one part are written on "Parchment Brand No. 3—12 Lines" paper. Remaining part (see Tizol, below) is on "Passantino Brand Number 1—12 Stave Medium" paper. Williams labeled the parts for many of the performers she anticipated would play them, including: "Pro" (Russell Procope, Alto Saxophone 1), "Rab" (Johnny Hodges, Alto Saxophone 2), "Jimmy" (Jimmy Hamilton, Tenor Saxophone 1, Clarinet), "Sears" (Al Sears, Tenor Saxophone 2), "Carney" (Harry Carney, Baritone Saxophone), "Brown" (Lawrence Brown, Trombone 1), "Jones" (Claude Jones, Trombone 2), "Tizol" (Juan Tizol, Trombone 2), "Wilbur" (Wilbur De Paris, Trombone 3), Guitar, Bass, Drums.

(2) MLWC: Incomplete score in Williams's hand on "King Brand No. 35" paper. Score is missing p. 5 (mm. 33–40), which in November 1994 was reconstructed and added by Mark Lopeman, based on the existing parts. Instruments include: Alto Saxophone 1–2, Tenor Saxophone 1–2, Baritone Saxophone, Trumpets 1–4, Trombones 1–3, Guitar, Piano, Bass, Drums.

(3) MLWC: Incomplete set of parts in Williams's hand on "King Brand No. 1" paper. Parts include: 1st Alto (Alto Saxophone 1), 3rd Alto (Alto Saxophone 2), I Tenor (Tenor Saxophone 1), II Tenor (Tenor Saxophone 2), 1st Trpt (Trumpet 1), 3rd Trpt (Trumpet 3), 4th Trpt (Trumpet 4), Trom (Trombone 1), II Trombone (Trombone 2), III Trombone (Trombone 3), Bass, Drums.

The score comprising the primary source is the only complete source extant. Each of the secondary sources (two sets of parts, one score) is incomplete. Yet secondary source (1), a set of parts, correlates closely with the primary source, and the other score and set of parts correlate closely too. The first pair proves to be a more complete and fully developed source. Delivered to Duke Ellington and his orchestra in the form of a score for an ensemble with five trumpets (not four) plus a number of parts written with specific band members in mind and catalogued as composition #237 in Ellington's library, suggesting that it belonged to the band's working repertory, it seems to represent the composer's last word on *Lonely Moments*. On the other hand, even as Williams supplied Ellington with the version of her newest work she deemed most polished, it may be that the pair of sources in the Mary Lou Williams Collection at the Institute of Jazz Studies were held back by their composer.

Intro/1, Tpt 1: "Harold," a reference to trumpeter Harold Baker, to whom Williams was married and who played in Duke Ellington's orchestra beginning in the fall of 1942 (Baker continued to play in Ellington's orchestra, off and on, through 1962).

Intro/1: Metronome markings throughout arrangement are conjectural. The recordings of this composition vary widely with respect to tempo: Goodman recorded his arrangement at ♩ = 164, while the Orent-Roth arrangement is recorded at ♩ = 142. The recent recording of this arrangement made by the Dutch Jazz Orchestra is much faster, at ♩ = 200.

Intro/5, all: "slow down."

A1/3.4, Trbs: no fall.

A1/9–15: "Copy 1 thru 7 of A" (here A1/1–7).

A1/11.4, Trbs: no fall.

A1/18.2, TSax 1: e♭″ (doubling of ASax 2) likely an error; here c″ (concert b♭′) suggested, 7th of C7♭9 not scored in any other Sax.

A1/19.1, TSax 1: b′, conflicts with Fm(maj7); here corrected to b♭′.

A1/20.1, TSax 2: e♭′, conflicts with Fm(maj7); here corrected to e′.

A1/25–31, Saxes, Trbs, Gtr, Pn, B, Dr: shorthand markings in each measure to copy "1A," "2A," etc., up to "7A" (here A1/1–7).

X/4.3, Saxes: rest missing as grace note is counted with an eighth-note value.

A2/1–31, Tpt 1: written-out solo (in A2/1–2) followed by a sequence of whole- and half-note block chords; here replaced with the modern practice of slash notation and chord symbols. From A2/3–9, the chords indicated in the score are (pitches from bottom to top): c′+e♭′+g♭′+a♭′, d♭′+f′+g′+b′, d♭′+e♭′+g′+b′, b+d′+f′+a′, c′+e♭′+g′+b′, c′+f′+a♭′+b♭′, d♭′+f′+g′+b′, c′+e♭′+g′+b′+d″. A2/10 uses a one-measure repeat sign. A2/11–14 use shorthand markings in each measure to copy "3C," "4C," … "6C." A2/15 contains two chords, both a+c′+e♭′+g′. From A2/17–23, the chords indicated in the score are: f′+a♭′+c″+e♭″, g′+a♭′+c″+e♭″, f′+a♭′+c″+e♭″, g′+a♭′+b♭′+c″+e♭″, g′+a′+b′+d″+f″. A2/24 uses a one-measure repeat sign. A2/25–29 use shorthand markings in each measure to copy "1C," "2C," … "5C." A2/30 contains g′+b′+d♭″+f″+a″. A2/31 contains g′+a′+c″+e♭″.

A2/9–14, Gtr, Pn, B, Dr: shorthand markings in each measure to copy "1C," "2C," … "6C" (here A2/1–7).

A2/25–29, Gtr: shorthand markings in each measure to copy "1C," "2C," … "5C" (here A2/1–5).

B/1: key signature change in Tpt 1 only. The changes for other instrumental families are at B/24 (Tpts 2–5), C/6 (Saxes), C/12 (Trbs), and D/1 (rhythm section).

B/1–23, Tpt 1, Dr: blank measures; here slash notation provided. Williams leaves the solo deliberately open in the score. On the Dutch Jazz Orchestra recording the Clarinet (rather than Trumpet) improvises around an extended Gm7 chord. This is consistent with the corresponding passage in the recordings Goodman made of this composition (the arrangement for Goodman also contained an open solo on an extended Gm7 chord, which Goodman himself played).

D/1, Saxes: quintuplet figure followed by dotted half note.

D/2.5–6, TSax 1: slur.

D/9–13: "Copy 1 of I . . . Copy 5 of I" (here D/1–5).

D/14, Tpts: "6 of I" (here D/6).

D/17.4, B: quarter note.

D/21.1, Tpt 1: no glissando.

IN THE LAND OF OO-BLA-DEE (1949)

For Dizzy Gillespie. Transcription from Recording

Composer.   Mary Lou Williams

Lyricist.   Milton Orent

Primary Source.   Recording: Victor LPV-530, matrix D9VB1796, reissued as BMG Music/Victor Jazz 09026-68517-2 (compact disc, 1996)

Date of Composition.   Uncertain; probably 1949

Date and Location of Recording.   6 July 1949, New York City

Band.   Dizzy Gillespie and His Orchestra

Personnel.   Dizzy Gillespie, Benny Harris, Elmon Wright, Willie Cook, trumpets; Andy Duryea, J. J. Johnson, Charles Greenlea, trombones; John Brown, Ernie Henry, alto saxophones; Joe Gayles, Yusef Lateef, tenor saxophones; Al Gibson, baritone saxophone; James Forman, piano; Al McKibbon, bass; Teddy Stewart, drums; Joe Carroll, vocalist

Form.   Key E♭: Intro$_{(7)}$ A1$_{(V, 4+4+6=14)}$ A2$_{(V, 14)}$ A3$_{(V, 14)}$ A4$_{(V, 14)}$ X$_{(2)}$ A5$_{(Tpt, 14)}$ A6$_{(V, 15)}$

For Dizzy Gillespie, a leader of the new jazz style known as bebop that emerged in 1940s New York, the big band remained a vital creative medium. Bebop is most closely associated with smaller groups, yet Gillespie worked to adapt the melodic, harmonic, and rhythmic techniques of this innovative style to the instrumentation of the big band. By the time of this composition, he had also collaborated with Cuban percussionist Chano Pozo on several occasions and explored the fusion of Cuban rhythmic elements with bebop style. It is assumed that Mary Lou Williams composed the Latin introduction along with the rest of this arrangement; as a personal friend of Gillespie, she would have known of his enthusiasms, and she tailored this introduction to fit them. Like her arrangement of *Lonely Moments, In the Land of Oo-Bla-Dee* is filled with many standard bebop traits: disjunct melodic lines, complex and often dissonant harmonies, and varied, unexpected background hits and rhythmic figures. As discussed in the essay, Williams studied musical structure and harmony informally with Orent in the mid-1940s and the two formed a friendship out of which this collaboration was born. Williams's structure for this composition, like Orent's lyrics, is strophic, telling a story over five verses (with no chorus). The narrative is interrupted only once (A5), for an improvised trumpet solo by Gillespie over the same fourteen-bar chord progression that undergirds all of the other verses.

IN THE LAND OF OO-BLA-DEE
(1 9 4 9)

222

met a beau- ti- ful prin- - cess in the land___ of Oo- Bla- Dee.___

E♭⁶   Fm⁷   E♭⁶ Fm⁷ E♭⁷   E♭⁷♯¹¹

Mary Lou Williams

Mary Lou Williams

Mary Lou Williams

IN THE LAND OF OO-BLA-DEE (1949)

Mary Lou Williams

Mary Lou Williams

Mary Lou Williams

Mary Lou Williams

In the Land of Oo-Bla-Dee (1949)

237

Mary Lou Williams

Mary Lou Williams

Mary Lou Williams

Mary Lou Williams

Mary Lou Williams

CRITICAL COMMENTARY

Secondary Sources. (1) MLWC: Piano/vocal sheet music, published 1949, Criterion Music Co., with red cover featuring a photo of Williams and inscription "Capitol Songs" in left corner. The top of the cover reads: "(In the Land of) Oo-Bla-Dee | Words and Music by Mary Lou Williams and Milton Orent | Recorded on King Records by Mary Lou Williams | Recorded on Capitol Records by Benny Goodman." Missing lyrics for third verse.

(2) MLWC: A score in Williams's hand also exists, but it bears the words "based off Dizzy Gillespie's Victor recording" across the top of the first page, indicating that it was written down after the fact, rather than being the recording's original score. The notation of the score also suggests that she sought to simplify aspects of the arrangement. A comparison of the score to the recording reveals many differences that bear out this hypothesis. This score has not been used for the transcription presented here.

On the recording, vocalist Joe Carroll takes many liberties with both pitches and rhythms in his interpretation. I have notated the vocal line in the score similarly to the "normalized" version found in the secondary source (1). However, since Carroll sings sometimes ahead of or behind the beat, differences such as duration of pitches and exact rhythmic position between the secondary source and my transcribed version occur, as I am transcribing (and thereby interpreting) the actual recording. Such differences are not reported in the critical notes. The pitch material of the vocal line differs only once from secondary source (1). I have settled for the pitch a♮′ in A1/7 and all repetitions of this motive (instead of the b♭′ found in the sheet music), as Carroll hits the former more often than the latter. I include a critical note each time the vocalist sings a variant on the here-notated "stricter" version. For verses 1, 2, 4, and 5 the edition follows the lyrics found in the secondary source. Any changes to these lyrics (other than modernizing the punctuation) are reported in the critical notes. Lower- and uppercase letters were adjusted without comment. The lyrics for the third verse are not included in the sheet music.

Critical Notes

Intro/1–7: though I have labeled arrangement as *Medium Swing*, introduction has Latin influences, including straight eighth-note playing in Saxes and pseudo-clave rhythm (2-3) in the Pn chord voicings supported by bass line in Intro/1–2.

Intro/6, Tpts, Trbs: brass players not quite together on this figure, particularly Intro/6.5–8, even though it appears to be a unison gesture (with octave duplication).

A1/1.7–2.1, V: b♭′; since tritone motive appears frequently, and on other occasions vocalist's pitch is closer to a′, pitch was made consistent.

A1/8.4–5, V: two eighth notes d♭″ in freely treated rhythm, slightly ahead of beat.

A1/9.2, lyrics: "bo."

A1/10.5, lyrics: "oo."

A2/1.4, lyrics: "right."

A2/3 and 6, Pn: instruction "play 1x, comp 2x" and chord symbols here provided to reflect recording, in which pianist plays notated figure the first time, but comps (accompanies) via chords the second time.

A2/5.4–6.1, V: 5.4–6 treated as quarter-note triplet and 5.7–6.1 shortened to 6.1.

A2/6.4–5, V: starts one eighth note earlier; eighth note d♭″ on 6.5 tied over into 7.1.

A2/8.4–5, V: d♭″–b♭′.

A2/10.4, V: c♭″.

A3/7, V: passage slightly behind beat.

A3/8.3–5, V: quarter-note triplet, with quarter rest and quarter notes d♭″–d♭″.

A3/10.1–3, V: quarter note followed by two eighth notes.

A3/10.4–5, V: eighth notes c♭″–c♭″.

A4/1.4, lyrics: "right."

A4/7.1–4, V: passage slightly behind beat.

A4/8, Saxes: not quite together in unison passage.

A4/8.3–5, V: quarter-note triplet, with quarter rest and quarter notes d♭″–d♭″.

A4/10, second half of measure, V: quarter-note triplet g♭′–c♭″–c♭″.

X/1.3, Tpts, Trbs, Pn, B, Dr: rhythm-section instruments play on afterbeat of beat 2, while brass play on beat 3; here rhythmically aligned.

A5, Tpt 4: improvisation by Dizzy Gillespie.

A5/2–4, Tpt 4: Gillespie consistently back-phrases, as if in a constant state of catching up; here notated on beat.

A5/7.4–6, Tpt 4: almost quarter-note triplet.

A5/11.9, Tpt 4: Gillespie arrives at the a♭′ early and seems to play it twice, almost as triplet b♭′–a♭′–a♭′.

A6/5.3–7.5, V: pitch and rhythm treated quite freely.

A6/8.3–4, V: quarter-note triplet, with quarter rest and quarter notes d♭″–d♭″.

A6/9.6–7, V: lyrics: "bee-doo."

A6/10.4–6, V: quarter-note triplet g♭′–c♭″–c♭″.

A6/14.2–5, Saxes: not quite together in unison passage.

GRAVEL (TRUTH) (1967)

For Duke Ellington. Edited from Manuscript

Composer.   Mary Lou Williams

Primary Source.   Autograph score in Williams's hand. Mary Lou Williams Collection, Institute of Jazz Studies, Rutgers University, Newark, NJ

Date of Composition.   Uncertain; probably 1967 (sent to Ellington, see p. lvii)

Recordings.   No studio recording of this composition was made in Williams's lifetime. A performance with Mary Lou Williams herself at the piano was given on a radio broadcast in 1968 by the Danish Radio Jazz Orchestra in Copenhagen, Denmark. A copy of this broadcast is archived in the Mary Lou Williams Collection, Institute of Jazz Studies, Rutgers University, Newark, NJ. A recording was made in 2005 by the Dutch Jazz Orchestra, Challenge Records CR73251 (compact disc)

Form.   Key D♭: $\text{Intro}_{(\text{ASax}, 5)}$ $\text{A1}_{(8)}$ $\text{A2}_{(8)}$ $\text{B1}_{(8)}$ $\text{A3}_{(9)}$ $\text{B2}_{(8)}$ $\text{A4}_{(8)}$ $\text{Tag}_{(3)}$

This arrangement represents a major revision of a composition Williams had written nearly thirty years earlier. It was recorded by Andy Kirk and His Twelve Clouds of Joy in 1940 as *Scratchin' in the Gravel*, a medium swing dance number. Here, Williams reconceives the song as a lush ballad, rich with thick, colorful harmonies and with a melody to be played by a solo alto saxophone. That she intended this arrangement for the Duke Ellington Orchestra is made clear by her labeling the second alto saxophone part in the score (the primary source) and in the corresponding set of parts (the secondary source) with the name "Johnny Hodges," referring to Ellington's featured alto saxophone soloist. The Ellington orchestra may have performed the piece, but they never recorded it. A performance was given on a radio broadcast in 1968 by the Danish Radio Jazz Orchestra in Copenhagen, Denmark, where Williams had been invited to headline the opening of a jazz club. The broadcast performance of the Danish Radio Jazz Orchestra presents the material as in the corrected score, which is used as the primary source here.

G R A V E L (T R U T H)
(1 9 6 7)

Mary Lou Williams

Mary Lou Williams

G R A V E L   (T R U T H)   (1 9 6 7)

Mary Lou Williams

Mary Lou Williams

Mary Lou Williams

Mary Lou Williams

G R A V E L   (T R U T H)   (1 9 6 7)

CRITICAL COMMENTARY

Primary Source. MLWC: Autograph score in Williams's hand on "Passantino Brands Eye Ease Score No. 1" paper. The score is in oblong format with sixteen staves per page and consists of eight pages. The paper provides a "Title" line at the top left, a "Page No." line at the top right and an "Arranger" line at the bottom. The title line reads "Gravel (Truth)," and, added in different hand, "= TRUTH." In addition the top bears the number "M. 386." The arranger line reads "Mary Lou Williams," in her hand. The autograph shows one layer of corrections with a thicker pencil, presumably by Williams herself. The corrections are not taken over in the set of parts, mentioned below. This edition follows the corrected score but gives notice of these corrections in the critical notes. Williams provides two continuous measure counts that do not correspond to each other: one at the top left side of each page, using circled or boxed measure numbers (spanning mm. 1–57, already included in the corrections), and another at the bottom, starting after the introduction (which has measures labeled A, B, C, D, and E) with m. 1 (corresponding to m. 6 circled at the top left of the second score page). Williams also gives section labels, which correspond to those of the present edition as follows: A = A1, B = A2, C = B1, D = B2.

Instrumentation. Alto Saxophones 1–2 (Alto 2 is labeled "Johnny Hodges"), Tenor Saxophones 1–2, Baritone Saxophone, Trumpets 1–4, Trombones 1–3, Piano, Bass, Drums.

Secondary Source. DEC: Incomplete autograph set of parts in Williams's hand, missing the drum part. All but one part on "King Brand 10 Stave/Glenn-Orent Music Service" paper. Additional part (see Johnny Hodges) is on "Passantino Brand—12 Stave Medium" paper. Parts are labeled: Alto (Alto 1), "Johnny Hodges" (Alto 2), 1st Tenor (Tenor 1), 2nd Tenor (Tenor 2), Baritone, Trumpets 1–4, Trombones 1–3, Piano, Bass.

Critical Notes

Intro/2 and 5, ASax 2: marked "cadenza"; here moved to beginning of each phrase.

Intro/4.5–6, ASax 2: g♯″–g″.

Intro/5.1, Trbs, Pn, B, Dr: fermata, here moved to Intro/4.

A1/1, B: *pizz.* marking conjectural, based on context and stylistic probability. Also reflected in the Danish Radio Jazz Orchestra broadcast.

A1/1–6, Dr: "Time" in drum part and single squiggly line. The drummer is to provide basic swing rhythm.

A1/4.3, ASax 1, TSaxes, Trbs: unclear marking; appears like a staccato dot, but interpreted as accent. Parts show no marking here, and very few elsewhere.

A1/4.5–8, ASax 1, TSaxes, Trbs: on broadcast recording eighth notes played as written, not swung.

A1/5.2–3, Tpt 4: rests missing.

A1/5.4, ASax 1, TSax 1: eighth rest missing.

A1/8: "NO REPEAT" over top staff.

A1/8, Tpt 2: "col Tpt 1."

A2/1–7, Dr: "Time" in drum part and single squiggly line. The drummer is to provide basic swing rhythm.

A2/2.2, Pn (RH): mistaken e′ in F7♯9.

A2/4.4, Pn (RH): g♭ and c′ missing (also missing in part).

A2/5.1, Pn (RH): B7♯9 chord symbol crossed out and replaced by Fø7. Though these chords share two common notes (b and d♭/c♯), the chord as voiced in the horn parts confirms the substituted chord symbol as correct. Chord voicing presented here is conjectural.

A2/6–7, TSax 2, BSax: shorthand "col 11 … 12" indicates that notes to be played are same as A1/6–7, minus the quarter-note triplet in A1/7.2–4. Shorthand notation and upbeat preceding it is not reflected in parts.

A2/8.1, Pn (RH): above "Dmaj7" is added "b?" in a hand not Williams's. Part has Dmaj7. Here Dma7 interpreted as a mistake and changed to D♭ma7 as LH has d♭.

A2/8.3, Pn (RH): notated as two tied eighth-note chords. In first chord lowest note not positioned clearly; here interpreted as f′ (part shows g′); in second chord b′ and f′ missing (also missing in part).

A2/8.4–B1/1.2, BSax: a♭′ corrected to e♭′ in primary source.

B1/3.1, TSax 1: a″ corrected to g″ in primary source.

B1/3.1, BSax: *8va* symbol added to f′ as correction in primary source.

B1/3.1, Trb 1: ♮ corrected with ♭ to b♭ in primary source.

B1/3.1, Trb 2: g corrected to f in primary source.

B1/3.2–4.1, Trb 3: pair of notes A♭–B♭ parallel to Trb 1, 2 crossed out in primary source.

B1/4, Saxes: ASax 1 shows quarter note, then no rests, and a quarter note at the end of the measure (part adds the two missing quarter rests); ASax 2 shows dotted half note and quarter note (part corresponds); TSax 1 shows half note, quarter rest, half rest, and quarter note (part has no half rest); TSax 2 shows quarter note, quarter rest, and half rest, and the next measure B1/6 starts with a "col" indication (part corresponds in B1/4 and writes out measures starting in B1/5, but without upbeat); BSax shows half note, quarter rest, half rest (part corresponds). Here measures regularized in all Saxes.

B1/5–7, TSax 2: "col," meaning with TSax 1.

B1/7.2–8.1, TSax 2: part shows mistaken tie from one d♭″ to another.

B1/8, Tpts 3–4: "col," meaning with Tpts 1–2.

B1/8.3, Pn: specific chord voicing provided in the part, with a♭+b♭+c′+e′ in the RH and an added lower octave in the LH.

B1/8.4, B: tenuto.

A3/2.1–4, Pn (RH): specific chord voicings provided in the part (g+d♭′+g♭′, a♭+d′+ g′, a+e♭′+a♭′, b♭+e′+a′).

A3/5–7, ASax 1, TSaxes, BSax, Tpts, Trbs: "col 10 11 12," correction/revision in primary source indicating that notes should be same as A1/5–7 (with the quarter-note triplet visible in light, possibly erased pencil markings on the primary source).

A3/8.3, Tpt 1: *f.*

A3/9: primary source revises 6/4 measure to 2/4 with annotation "everybody half note."

B2: metronome marking is conjectural, derived from recording by Danish Radio Jazz Orchestra.

B2/1.2–7 and 2.2–7, TSax 2: "col," meaning with TSax 1.

B2/1–6, Tpts 2–4: "col Tpt 1."

B2/1–6, B: measures with rests; part shows an added annotation "play" over notated seven measures of rest (B2/4 consists of two 3/4 measures in the part set; a correction in the score reads "one bar"). A 1968 recording with the Danish Radio Jazz Orchestra at which Williams was present indicates that she intended the bass to walk freely over the chord changes.

B2/2.1, TSax 2: a♭′ corrected to c″ in primary source.

B2/5–6, Saxes: before revision of primary source it read (only deviations from B2/1–2 are listed): ASax 2, B2/5.6–7 and 6.6–7: d♭‴–e♭‴; TSax 1, B2/6.1: g″ (an earlier e″ was erased), B2/5.6–7 and 6.6–7: e♭″–f″; TSax 2, B2/6.1: a♭′.

B2/6.6, Tpts 3–4: c‴ as instruction "Col Tpt 1" calls for; here changed to c″ to maintain common tone across barline to 7.1.

B2/7–8.7, Tpt 2: "col," meaning with Tpt 1.

B2/7–8.7, Tpt 4: "col," meaning with Tpt 3.

B2/8.1, BSax, Trb, Pn, B: note was first written as half note followed by another pitch or rest, then corrected by adding dot to half note and crossing out the following pitch/rest. In BSax rest was not crossed out.

B2/8.1, Pn (RH): dotted half note b♭′, eighth note b♭′, dotted quarter note b′. Here substituted with slash notation as placeholder for chord, for which symbol is provided. It is not clear whether pitch in primary source is meant to be chord's top note.

B2/8.5, ASax 2: "Alto takes pickup after cutoff (write this in his part!)."

A4/1–6: notation of Saxes, Tpts, Trbs crossed out and instead "All Horns col 14 15 16 17 18 19" (measure numbers overwriting the ASax Solo reading "9 10 11 12 13 14"), meaning repeat of measures A2/1–6, except for TSax 2, BSax A2/6 with upbeat, which should be left out ("except Tenors Tacit Here / Bari Tacit Here"—the "Tacit Here" for BSax is crossed out and quarter note added to end of measure).

A4/7–8, B: a tie that appeared across the barline between these two measures was crossed out in a correction.

A4/8, Pn (LH): no note.

Tag/1.8, BSax: no glissando.

Tag/2–3, Tpts: Williams seems first to have written two tied whole notes for the last two measures. This is reflected in the parts. Then she revised Tpts 1–3 to a half note. In Tpt 4, however, neither the tie nor the note in the last measure is crossed out, and a stem on the note in the penultimate measure is scribbled out. This edition treats all Tpts the same with a half note in the penultimate measure. The Danish Radio Jazz Orchestra broadcast, however, presents the ending with tied whole notes for all trumpets.

Tag/2–3, Dr: tied, rolled whole notes appear in the top space. Williams likely intended a roll on the ride cymbal. Here these whole notes are moved to the top line per conventional notation (see pp. lxvi–lxvii).

ARIES MOOD (1968)

For Danish Radio Jazz Orchestra. Edited from Manuscript

Composer. Mary Lou Williams

Primary Source. Autograph score in Williams's hand. Mary Lou Williams Collection, Institute of Jazz Studies, Rutgers University, Newark, NJ

Date of Composition. 1968, according to inscription on score

Recordings. No studio recording of this composition exists from Williams's lifetime. A performance with Mary Lou Williams herself at the piano was given on a radio broadcast in 1968 by the Danish Radio Jazz Orchestra in Copenhagen, Denmark. A copy of this broadcast is archived in the Mary Lou Williams Collection, Institute of Jazz Studies, Rutgers University, Newark, NJ. A recording was made in 2005 by the Dutch Jazz Orchestra, Challenge Records CR73251 (compact disc)

Form. Key B♭: $Intro_{(17)} X_{(2)} A1_{(16)} A2_{(ASax, 16)} B1_{(12)} B2_{(Fl, 12)} C_{(TSax, Bass, Fl, 14+16=30)} Tag_{(3)}$

Williams conceived this piece as an "avant-garde blues" (so labeled on the score).[1] Though she does not define this label, the composition's sudden shifts of mood, tempo, and tonality, as well as passages that fit uneasily into the twelve-bar blues structure, explain her characterization. These traits also fit well with those generally attributed to the sign of the zodiac known as Aries, which include aggressiveness, impulsiveness, assertiveness, and spontaneity. Subtitled "A Portrait of Ben Webster," it was most likely written with tenor saxophonist Webster in mind, for he performed with the Danish Radio Jazz Orchestra on their broadcast of the piece in 1968. Though Williams's own notation indicates a title of simply *Aries*, her longtime manager and the current Executive Director of the Mary Lou Williams Foundation, Peter O'Brien, maintains (through private correspondence) that she referred to the piece as *Aries Mood*.

---

1. See also introductory essay for a discussion of this piece, pp. lvii–lix.

ARIES MOOD

(1 9 6 8)

ARIES MOOD (1968)

Mary Lou Williams

Mary Lou Williams

Mary Lou Williams

ARIES MOOD (1968)

278

Mary Lou Williams

Mary Lou Williams

ARIES MOOD (1968)

CRITICAL COMMENTARY

Primary Source.   MLWC: Autograph score in Williams's hand, on "Passantino #9" paper. The score is in oblong format with eighteen staves per page and consists of fourteen pages (eight predrawn measures per page). The paper provides a "Composition" (Title) line at the top left and a "Page" line at the top right. The composition line reads "Aries (very fast)." In addition, the top bears the signature "Mary Lou Williams— Arranger and Composer," and a descriptive phrase that reads "Dedicated to Billy [*sic*] Holiday—Bop Avante [*sic*] Blues." Additionally, various identifying markings appear on a cover page: in Williams's hand, "Aries 1968" is written and circled. Adjacent to this is "M3895," as is "Arr. and Composed by Mary Lou Williams" and the words "Send page 1 of score to Karlton." "G416" is stamped on the cover page in black ink, and "DANMARKS RADIO Nodebiblioteket" ("Denmark Radio Music Library") is stamped in red ink. Rusted staples along the top, middle, and bottom of the left side of each page appear to have bound the score at one time, though some score pages have come loose. Williams provides a continuous measure count at the bottom using circled measure numbers (spanning mm. 1–80, corresponding to pp. 1–10, after which measure numbers are cut off or, when they do appear, are incorrect). Williams labels the sections, starting after the Intro, in a way corresponding to the present edition as follows: A = X/A1/A2; B = B1; C = B2; and D = C/Tag.

Instrumentation.   Alto Saxophones 1–2 (Alto 2 also doubles with flute), Tenor Saxophones 1–2, Baritone Saxophone, Trumpets 1–4, Trombones 1–3, Bass, Piano, Drums.

Secondary Source.   MLWC: Score in unknown copyist's hand, on unidentifiable, eleven-staff paper in portrait format.

Critical Notes

Intro/1–4, Pn: notation in bass clef only, with stems in both directions and instruction "both hands"; here interpreted as meant to be played an octave apart.

Intro/1–17, ASax 2: "col," meaning with ASax 1.

Intro/1–17, TSax 2: "col," meaning with TSax 1.

Intro/3.3, BSax: c♭″.

Intro/5, BSax, Tpts: half rest in second half of measure missing.

Intro/5, Trbs, B, Pn: second half of measure corrects eighth and quarter rest to half rest.

Intro/5, Dr: too many beats in measure; snare drum has triplet of eighths, dotted eighth, eighth, sixteenth, accented eighth, eighth rest, and quarter slash; bass drum has quarter note, quarter note, eighth note, eighth rest, quarter note.

Intro/8.4, Pn (RH): e♮′; here corrected to match Tpt 4.

Intro/9.1, Pn: bottom note of chord missing; here added as preceding chords have been four-note, mostly quartal harmonies.

Intro/9.8, ASaxes: a♯′; missing ♮ signs for unison line in Saxes; see comment at Intro/10.5.

Intro/10.5, TSaxes: c‴; missing ♯ signs for unison line in Saxes. Since all Saxes require accidentals, it is more likely that accidentals are missing than that accidentals for ASaxes were wrongly provided.

Intro/11.9, ASaxes: c♯′; missing ♮ signs.

Intro/17.6, TSaxes: e″; error based on Saxes' unison line; corrected to align with ASaxes. But an alternative—TSaxes are correct and ASaxes incorrect—is also possible.

X/1.5–6 and A1/1.5–6, B: dotted eighth note and sixteenth note. Because eighth notes in a "slow swing" style are usually performed with a swing feel, the rhythmic notation has been simplified.

A1/4–A2/16, Dr: blank measures, except for a one-bar figure and instruction "fill in" in A2/10–11. Since it is unlikely that drums are to drop out here, a four-beat swing rhythm is provided.

A2/5.9–16, ASax 1: repeat sign to indicate repetition of A2/5.1–8, even though rhythmic figures in first two beats add up to too many beats. Accordingly, the lengths of f‴ at A2/5.3–4 (quarter note) and g″ at A2/5.7–8 (quarter note) are adjusted.

A2/8–11, TSaxes: "Bend"; replaced by "*sim.*"

A2/10–11, Trbs 2–3: "Bend"; replaced by "*sim.*"

A2/10.1, Tpt 3: possibly b″.

B1/1–12, Pn (RH): blank measures and word "Piano" in B1/1; here slash notation is added and chord symbols provided where bass ostinato changes for pianist to fill in with improvised melody or chord accompaniment. In broadcast recording by Danish Radio Jazz Orchestra, with Mary Lou Williams herself playing piano, rather than doubling bass line with her left hand, she provides extremely sparse comping throughout this passage.

B1/1.1–2, B: eighth note followed by half rest; here adjusted to half note to correspond with piano.

B1/1–B2/11, Dr: blank measures and instruction "play with Bass – fill in." Interpreted to mean that drummer is to fill these measures with the continued slow swing rhythms and additional hits and fills around the bass ostinato and with the Fl solo; slash notation provided here.

B1/1.5, B: tenuto.

B2/1–12, Fl: blank measures; here replaced by slash notation and an inferred A♭7 chord symbol (from the bass's ostinato figure).

B2/1–12, Pn: blank measures; here replaced by tied half note a♭ at B2/1.1 (for consistency with pattern completed by B), slash notation, and instruction "comp/fill over A♭7" (inferred from the bass's ostinato figure). In the broadcast recording, Williams comps sparsely behind flute solo.

B2/2.4–6, TSax 1: no triplet sign.

B2/3.3–4, B: e♭–f.

B2/4.2–12.4, B: blank measures and instruction "Play same rythm [*sic*] pattern"; here replaced by music notation. In B2/12 it is unclear how Williams intends bass to navigate transition into C.

C/1–30, B: blank measures; here replaced by slash notation and instruction "free over A♭7," based on lengthy ostinato centered on A♭ preceding this passage.

C/1–30, Dr: some blank measures; here replaced by slash notation (indicating standard swing rhythms).

C/7–30, TSax 1: blank measures with instructions "Tenor" at C/7 and "Tenor Solo" at C/14 and C/22; here blank measures replaced by slash notation and inferred "free over B♭7" instruction (consistent with bass solo continuing over A♭7).

C/14–30, Fl: blank measures with instruction "Flute Solo" at C/14 and C/22; here blank measures replaced by slash notation and inferred "free over A♭7" instruction (consistent with bass solo continuing over A♭7).

Tag/1–3, Fl: "col" (indicating that Fl is to play in unison with ASax 1).

BIBLIOGRAPHY

Unpublished Archival Sources

Mary Lou Williams Collection, Institute of Jazz Studies, Rutgers University, Newark, NJ (MLWC)

Music

Williams, Mary Lou. *Aries Mood* (1968). Primary and secondary source material for this edition.

———. *Gravel (Truth)* (1967). Primary source material for this edition.

———. *Lonely Moments* (1947). Secondary source material for this edition.

———. *Mary's Idea* (1938). Primary and secondary source material for this edition.

———. *A Mellow Bit of Rhythm* (1937). Primary and secondary source material for this edition.

———. *Messa Stomp* (1938). Primary and secondary source material for this edition.

———. *Scorpio* (1946). Secondary source material for this edition.

———. *In the Land of Oo-Bla-Dee* (1949). Secondary source material for this edition (see also "Musical Scores" section below for published sheet music found in the MLWC).

Articles, Letters

Thompson, Richard. "Mary Lou Williams: Zodiac Suite; A Critical Analysis." Undated academic paper.

Williams, Mary Lou. Carbon copy of letter to Duke Ellington, 21 August 1967.

Benny Goodman Papers, Irving S. Gilmore Music Library, Yale University, New Haven, CT (BGP)

Williams, Mary Lou. *A Mellow Bit of Rhythm* (1937), secondary source material for this edition.

———. *Lonely Moments* (1947). Version for Goodman's combo. Parts in Williams's hand.

Duke Ellington Collection, Smithsonian National Museum of American History Archives Center, Washington, D.C. (DEC)

Williams, Mary Lou. *Gravel (Truth)* (1968). Secondary source material for this edition.

———. *Lonely Moments* (1947). Primary and secondary source material for this edition.

———. *Scorpio* (1946). Primary and secondary source material for this edition.

Smithsonian National Museum of American History Archives Center, Washington, D.C.

Williams, Mary Lou. Interview by John S. Wilson. Transcript of tape recording, 26 June 1973. Smithsonian Institute Interviews with Jazz Musicians. *Jazz Oral History Project.*

PUBLISHED SOURCES

Books, Articles, Dissertations, Databases, Websites, Newspapers

Ake, David, ed. *Jazz Cultures*. Berkeley: University of California Press, 2002.
———. "Regendering Jazz: Ornette Coleman and the New York Scene in the Late 1950s." In *Jazz Cultures*, edited by David Ake, 62–82. Berkeley: University of California Press, 2002.
Balliett, Whitney. "Out Here Again." *The New Yorker* 40, no. 11, 2 May 1964.
Baraka, Amiri. *Blues People: Negro Music in White America*. New York: W. Morrow, 1963.
Berendt, Joachim. *The Jazz Book: From New Orleans to Rock and Free Jazz*. Translated by Dan Morgenstern and Barbara Bredigkeit. New York: L. Hill, 1975.
Berger, Morroe, Edward Berger, and James Patrick. *Benny Carter: A Life in American Music*. 2nd ed. Metuchen, NJ: Scarecrow Press, 2001.
Buehrer, Ted. "*Lonely Moments?* The Anatomy of Mary Lou Williams' Oft-Recorded Tune." *International Association of Jazz Educators Research Proceedings Yearbook* (January 2003): 52–63.
Chevan, David. "Written Music in Early Jazz." PhD diss., City University of New York, 1997.
Chilton, John. *McKinney's Music: A Bio-discography of McKinney's Cotton Pickers*. London: Bloomsbury Book Shop, 1978.
Collier, James Lincoln. *The Making of Jazz: A Comprehensive History*. Boston: Houghton Mifflin, 1978.
Crawford, Richard. *The American Musical Landscape: The Business of Musicianship from Billings to Gershwin*. Berkeley: University of California Press, 1993; 2000.
Dahl, Linda. *Morning Glory: A Biography of Mary Lou Williams*. New York: Pantheon Books, 1999.
———. *Stormy Weather: The Music and Lives of a Century of Jazzwomen*. New York: Pantheon Books, 1984.
DeVeaux, Scott. "Constructing the Jazz Tradition: Jazz Historiography." *Black American Literature Forum* 25 (1991): 525–60.
———. *The Birth of Bebop: A Social and Musical History*. Berkeley: University of California Press, 1997.
DeVeaux, Scott, and Gary Giddins. *Jazz*. New York: W. W. Norton, 2009.
Driggs, Frank, and Chuck Haddix. *Kansas City Jazz: From Ragtime to Bebop—A History*. New York: Oxford University Press, 2005.
Ellington, Duke. *Music Is My Mistress*. Garden City, NY: Doubleday, 1973.
Elworth, Steven B. "Jazz in Crisis, 1948–1958: Ideology and Representation." In *Jazz Among the Discourses*, edited by Krin Gabbard, 57–75. Durham: Duke University Press, 1995.
Feather, Leonard. *The Book of Jazz*. New York: Meridian Books, 1957.
Firestone, Ross. *Swing, Swing, Swing: The Life and Times of Benny Goodman*. New York: W. W. Norton, 1993.
Gabbard, Krin, ed. *Jazz Among the Discourses*. Durham: Duke University Press, 1995.
———, ed. *Representing Jazz*. Durham: Duke University Press, 1995.
———. "Signifyin(g) the Phallus: 'Mo' Better Blues' and Representations of the Jazz Trumpet." *Cinema Journal* 32, no. 1 (1992): 43–62. (Also in *Representing Jazz*, edited by Krin Gabbard, 104–30. Durham: Duke University Press, 1995.)

Theodore E. Buehrer

Giddins, Gary. "Mary Lou Williams: 1910–1981." *Village Voice*, 10 June 1981.

Gioia, Ted. *The History of Jazz*. 2nd ed. New York: Oxford University Press, 2011.

Givan, Benjamin Marx. "Django Reinhardt's Style and Improvisational Process." PhD diss., Yale University, 2003.

Gottlieb, Robert, ed. *Reading Jazz: A Gathering of Autobiography, Reportage, and Criticism from 1919 to Now*. New York: Vintage Books, 1999.

Gridley, Mark. *Jazz Styles*, 11th ed. Englewood Cliffs, NJ: Prentice Hall, 2011.

———. *Jazz Styles*. Englewood Cliffs, NJ: Prentice Hall, 1978.

Hairston, Monica. "Gender, Jazz, and the Popular Front." In *Big Ears: Listening for Gender in Jazz Studies*, edited by Nichole T. Rustin and Sherrie Tucker, 64–89. Durham: Duke University Press, 2008.

Handy, D. Antoinette. *Black Women in American Bands and Orchestras*. Metuchen, NJ: Scarecrow Press, 1981.

———. "Conversation with Mary Lou Williams, First Lady of the Jazz Keyboard." *Black Perspectives in Music* 8, no. 2 (1980): 194–214.

Harrison, Max. "Swing Era Big Bands and Jazz Composing and Arranging." In *The Oxford Companion to Jazz*, edited by Bill Kirchner, 277–91. New York: Oxford University Press, 2000.

Howland, John. "Between the Muses and the Masses: Symphonic Jazz, 'Glorified' Entertainment, and the Rise of the American Musical Middlebrow, 1920–1944 (Duke Ellington, James P. Johnson, Paul Whiteman)." PhD diss., Stanford University, 2002.

———. *Ellington Uptown: Duke Ellington, James P. Johnson, and the Birth of Concert Jazz*. Jazz Perspectives. Ann Arbor: University of Michigan Press, 2009.

———. "The Whitemanesque Roots of Early Ellingtonian 'Extended Jazz Composition.'" *International Association of Jazz Educators Research Proceedings Yearbook* (January 2003): 16–31.

Ingham, John N. *Biographical Dictionary of American Business Leaders*. Westport, CT: Greenwood Press, 1983.

"Jazz Pianist Mary Lou Williams Dead at 71." The Associated Press, 29 May 1981. LexisNexis Academic. www.lexisnexis.com/hottopics/lnacademic (accessed 15 May 2012).

Kelley, Robin D. G. *Thelonious Monk: The Life and Times of an American Original*. New York: Free Press, 2009.

Kernodle, Tammy. "Anything You Are Shows Up in Your Music: Mary Lou Williams and the Sanctification of Jazz." PhD diss., The Ohio State University, 1997.

———. *Soul on Soul: The Life and Music of Mary Lou Williams*. Boston: Northeastern University Press, 2004.

Kirchner, Bill, ed. *The Oxford Companion to Jazz*. New York: Oxford University Press, 2000.

Kirk, Andy, and Amy Lee. *Twenty Years on Wheels*. Ann Arbor: University of Michigan Press, 1989.

Larson, Steve. *Analyzing Jazz: A Schenkerian Approach*. Harmonologia: Studies in Music Theory 15. Hillsdale, NY: Pendragon, 2009.

Levine, Mark. *The Jazz Theory Book*. Petaluma, CA: Sher Music, 1995.

Lord, Tom. *The Jazz Discography* [CD-ROM]. West Vancouver, BC: Lord Music Reference, 1999.

Maddocks, Melvin. "A Celebrant of Jazz." *Christian Science Monitor*, 4 June 1981.

Magee, Jeffrey. "Before Louis: When Fletcher Henderson Was the 'Paul Whiteman of the Race.'" *American Music* 18, no. 4 (2000): 391–425.

———. "The Music of Fletcher Henderson and His Orchestra in the 1920s." PhD diss., University of Michigan, 1992.

———. *The Uncrowned King of Swing: Fletcher Henderson and Big Band Jazz*. New York: Oxford University Press, 2005.

Maher, James T., and Jeffrey Sultanof. "Pre-Swing Era Big Bands and Jazz Composing and Arranging." In *The Oxford Companion to Jazz*, edited by Bill Kirchner, 264–76. New York: Oxford University Press, 2000.

Martin, Henry. *Charlie Parker and Thematic Improvisation*. Studies in Jazz 24. Lanham, MD: Scarecrow, 2001.

Martin, Henry, and Keith Waters. *Jazz: The First 100 Years*. 3rd ed. Belmont, CA: Schirmer, 2011.

McPartland, Marian. "Mary Lou: Marian McPartland Salutes One Pianist Who Remains Modern and Communicative." *Downbeat* 24, no. 2, 17 October 1957, 12.

Monson, Ingrid. "The Problem with White Hipness: Race, Gender, and Cultural Conceptions in Jazz Historical Discourse." *Journal of the American Musicological Society* (1995): 396–422.

Morgenstern, Dan. Liner Notes. *Mary Lou Williams: The Zodiac Suite*. See section "Recordings" below.

Panassié, Hughes. *Hot Jazz: The Guide to Swing Music*. Translated by Lyle and Eleanor Dowling. New York: M. Witmark and Sons, 1936.

"Petrillo, James Caesar." In *Encyclopedia of Popular Music*, 4th ed., edited by Colin Larkin. *Oxford Music Online*. www.oxfordmusiconline.com (accessed 2 May 2012).

Pickeral, Charles Wilkins. "The Masses of Mary Lou Williams: The Evolution of a Liturgical Style." PhD diss., Texas Tech University, 1998.

Placksin, Sally. *American Women in Jazz: 1900 to the Present; Their Words, Lives, and Music*. New York: Wideview Books, 1982.

Rattenbury, Ken. *Duke Ellington: Jazz Composer*. New Haven: Yale University Press, 1990.

Rust, Brian. *Jazz Records: 1897–1942*. 5th ed. Chigwell, Essex, England: Storyville Publications, 1982.

Rustin, Nichole T., and Sherrie Tucker, eds. *Big Ears: Listening for Gender in Jazz Studies*. Refiguring American Music. Durham: Duke University Press, 2008.

Rye, Howard. "Wilson, Garland." In *The New Grove Dictionary of Jazz*, 2nd ed., edited by Barry Kernfeld. *Grove Music Online*. *Oxford Music Online*. www.oxfordmusiconline.com (accessed 15 June 2012).

Schuller, Gunther. *Early Jazz: Its Roots and Musical Development*. New York: Oxford University Press, 1986.

———. *The Swing Era: The Development of Jazz, 1930–1945*. New York: Oxford University Press, 1989.

Scott, Joan. "Gender: A Useful Category of Historical Analysis." *The American Historical Review* 91, no. 5 (1986): 1053–75.

Sheridan, Chris. *Brilliant Corners: A Bio-discography of Thelonious Monk*. Westport, CT: Greenwood Press, 2001.

Stearns, Marshall. *The Story of Jazz*. New York: Oxford University Press, 1956.

Tirro, Frank. *Jazz: A History*. 2nd ed. New York: W. W. Norton, 1993.

Tucker, Mark. *Ellington: The Early Years*. Music in American Life. Urbana: University of Illinois Press, 1991.

Tucker, Sherrie. "Big Ears: Listening for Gender in Jazz Studies." *Current Musicology* 71–73 (2001): 375–408.

———. "Historiography, jazz." In *The New Grove Dictionary of Jazz*, 2nd ed., edited by Barry Kernfeld. *Grove Music Online*. *Oxford Music Online*. www.oxfordmusiconline.com (accessed 9 August 2012, search "Historiography," *Grove Music Online*, then go to "archived articles").

———. *Swing Shift: "All-Girl" Bands of the 1940s*. Durham: Duke University Press, 2000.

Ulanov, Barry. *A History of Jazz in America*. New York: Viking Press, 1952.

van de Leur, Walter. *Something to Live For: The Music of Billy Strayhorn*. New York: Oxford University Press, 2002.

Vihlen, Elizabeth. "Jammin' on the Champs-Elysées: Jazz, France, and the 1950s." In *Here, There, and Everywhere: The Foreign Politics of American Popular Culture*, edited by Reinhold Wagnleitner and Elaine Tyler May, 149–62. Hanover, NH: University of New England Press, 2000.

———. "Sounding French: Jazz in Postwar France." PhD diss., State University of New York, Stony Brook, 2000.

Waters, Keith. *The Studio Recordings of the Miles Davis Quintet, 1965–68*. Oxford Studies in Recorded Jazz. New York: Oxford University Press, 2011.

Weinberg, Norman. *Guide to Standardized Drumset Notation*. Lawton, OK: Percussive Arts Society, 1998.

Williams, Martin. *The Jazz Tradition*. New York: Oxford University Press, 1970.

Williams, Mary Lou. "Autobiography." In *Reading Jazz: A Gathering of Autobiography, Reportage, and Criticism from 1919 to Now*, edited by Robert Gottlieb, 87–116. New York: Vintage Books, 1999.

Wilson, John S. "Mary Lou Williams: A Jazz Great, Dies." *The New York Times*, 30 May 1981, sec. Obituaries. http://www.nytimes.com/1981/05/30/obituaries/mary-lou-williams-a-jazz-great-dies.html (accessed 22 May 2012).

Youngren, William H. "European Roots of Jazz." In *The Oxford Companion to Jazz*, edited by Bill Kirchner, 17–28. New York: Oxford University Press, 2000.

Documentary Films

Mary Lou Williams: Music on My Mind. Joanne Burke (director). Roberta Flack (narrator). 60 min. 1990.

Mary Lou Williams: The Lady Who Swings the Band. Carol Bash (director). In post-production.

Musical Scores

Davis, Miles. *Birth of the Cool*, edited by Jeffrey Sultanof. Milwaukee, WI: Hal Leonard, 2002.

Hines, Earl "Fatha." *Selected Piano Solos, 1928–1941*, edited by Jeffrey Taylor. Music of the United States of America 15. Middleton, WI: A-R Editions, 2006.

Sam Morgan's Jazz Band. *Complete Recorded Works in Transcription*, edited by John J. Joyce Jr., Bruce Boyd Raeburn, and Anthony M. Cummings. Music of the United States of America 24. Middleton, WI: A-R Editions, 2012.

Waller, Thomas Wright "Fats." *Performances in Transcription, 1927–1943*, edited by Paul Machlin. Music of the United States of America 10. Middleton, WI: A-R Editions, 2001.

Williams, Mary Lou. *In the Land of Oo-Bla-Dee*. Piano/vocal sheet music, red cover. New York: Criterion Music Co., 1949. (Found in MLWC.)

———. *In the Land of Oo-Bla-Dee*. Piano sheet music, black cover. Be-bop Piano Solo Series. Piano Solo by Pete Rugolo. New York: Criterion Music Co., 1949. (Found in MLWC.)

———. *In the Land of Oo-Bla-Dee: Recorded by Dizzy Gillespie*. Full Score [transcription from recording]. Edited by Jeffrey Sultanof. (The Jeffrey Sultanof Master Edition.) Saratoga Springs, NY: Jazz Lines Publications, 2011. JLP-8785.

———. [Arranger]. *Lonely Moments: As Arranged for Duke Ellington*. Full Score from the Original Manuscript. Edited by Jeffrey Sultanof. (The Jeffrey Sultanof Master Edition.) Saratoga Springs, NY: Jazz Lines Publications, 2010. JLP-8776.

———. *Mary's Idea (1930): As Recorded by Andy Kirk*. Full Score [transcription from recording]. Edited by Jeffrey Sultanof. (The Jeffrey Sultanof Master Edition.) Saratoga Springs, NY: Jazz Lines Publications, 2010. JLP-8787.

———. *Mary's Idea (1938): Recorded by Andy Kirk*. Full Score [transcription from recording]. Edited by Jeffrey Sultanof. Saratoga Springs, NY: Jazz Lines Publications, 2010. JLP-8786.

————. *A Mellow Bit of Rhythm: Recorded by Andy Kirk.* Full Score [transcription from recording]. Edited by Rob Duboff and Jeffrey Sultanof. Saratoga Springs, NY: Jazz Lines Publications, 2012. JLP-8794.

————. *Messa Stomp (1929) [aka Mess A Stomp]: Recorded by Andy Kirk.* Full Score from the Original Manuscript [*sic*; correctly: transcription from recording]. Edited by Jeffrey Sultanof. Saratoga Springs, NY: Jazz Lines Publications, 2010. JLP-8779.

————. *Scorpio: As Arranged for Duke Ellington, 1946.* Full Score from the Original Manuscript. Edited by Jeffrey Sultanof. (The Jeffrey Sultanof Master Edition.) Saratoga Springs, NY: Jazz Lines Publications, 2010. JLP-8775.

————. *Walkin' and Swingin'.* Edited by Theodore Edward Buehrer. Jazz at Lincoln Center's Essentially Ellington Library. [Van Nuys, CA]: Belwin Jazz, 2009.

Williams, Mary Lou, and Herman Walder. *A Mellow Bit of Rhythm.* Radio City, NY: Leeds Music Co., 1940.

————. *A Mellow Bit of Rhythm.* London: Peter Maurice Music Co., 1944.

Recordings

Andy Kirk and His Twelve Clouds of Joy, 1929–1931. The Chronological Classics. Classics 655, 1992.

Andy Kirk and His Twelve Clouds of Joy, 1936–1937. The Chronological Classics. Classics 573, 1991.

Andy Kirk and His Twelve Clouds of Joy, 1937–1938. The Chronological Classics. Classics 581, 1991.

Andy Kirk and His Twelve Clouds of Joy, 1938. The Chronological Classics. Classics 598, 1991.

Andy Kirk and His Twelve Clouds of Joy, 1939–1940. The Chronological Classics. Classics 640, 1992.

Andy Kirk and His Clouds of Joy, 1940–1942. The Chronological Classics. Classics 681, 1993.

Benny Goodman: Undercurrent Blues. Capitol Jazz 7243-8-32086-2-3, 1995.

Benny Goodman and His Orchestra. Jazz Anthology. Musidisc LP 30JA5152.

Benny Goodman and His Rhythm Makers. Original 1935 Radio Transcriptions. Tax CD 3708-2.

Dizzy Gillespie: Dizzier and Dizzier. BMG Music/Victor Jazz 09026-68517-2, 1996.

Dizzy Gillespie: At Newport. Verve/Polygram 7476274, 1957.

Duke Ellington and His Orchestra, 1945. Vol. 1. Circle CCD-101.

Fletcher Henderson, 1932–1934. The Chronological Classics. Classics 535.

Glenn Miller Live! Reader's Digest. CD 3979.

The Jazz Collector Edition. Benny Goodman Orchestra. Laserlight 15762, 1991.

The Legacy of Mary Lou Williams. United States Army Field Band Jazz Ambassadors. Altissimo 62102, 2011.

Mary Lou Williams, 1927–1940. The Chronological Classics. Classics 630, 1996.

Mary Lou Williams, 1944. The Chronological Classics. Classics 814, 1995.

Mary Lou Williams, 1944–1945. The Chronological Classics. Classics 1021, 1998.

Mary Lou Williams, 1945–1947. The Chronological Classics. Classics 1050, 1999.

Mary Lou Williams, 1949–1951. The Chronological Classics. Classics 1260, 2002.

Mary Lou Williams, 1951–1953. The Chronological Classics. Classics 1346, 2004.

Mary Lou Williams: The Zodiac Suite. Jazz Classics Records JZCL-6002, 1999.

Mary Lou Williams: The Zodiac Suite. Liner Notes by Dan Morgenstern. Smithsonian/ Folkways SF CD 40810, 1995.

Mary's Idea. Andy Kirk and Mary Lou Williams. The Original Decca Recordings. GRP, GRD 622, 1993.

"Put it There." McKinney's Cotton Pickers. Volume 1928–29. Frog DGF 25, 1999.

Rediscovered Music of Mary Lou Williams, the Lady Who Swings the Band. Dutch Jazz Orchestra. Challenge Records CR73251, 2005.